T0178831

Time-Predictable Architectures

FOCUS SERIES

Series Editor Luis Farinas del Cerro

Time-Predictable Architectures

Christine Rochange
Sascha Uhrig
Pascal Sainrat

WILEY

First published 2014 in Great Britain and the United States by ISTE Ltd and John Wiley & Sons, Inc.

ISTE Ltd
27-37 St George's Road
London SW19 4EU
UK

www.iste.co.uk

John Wiley & Sons, Inc.
111 River Street
Hoboken, NJ 07030
USA

www.wiley.com

Library of Congress Control Number: 2013953947

British Library Cataloguing-in-Publication Data
A CIP record for this book is available from the British Library
ISSN 2051-2481 (Print)
ISSN 2051-249X (Online)
ISBN 978-1-84821-593-1

Printed and bound in Great Britain by CPI Group (UK) Ltd., Croydon, Surrey CR0 4YY

Contents

Preface

Computer systems are becoming increasingly powerful, but at the same time they are also becoming increasingly complex. Even though increased computing performance is intended in the core, the complexity raises major challenges, especially in the domain of hard real-time systems. These systems need to provide a deterministic timing behavior since unpredictable variations of timing can lead to catastrophic results.

This book is based on two habilitation theses of Christine Rochange and Sascha Uhrig, enriched with valuable expansions from Pascal Sainrat. It addresses processor architectures and tools as well as software developers with the intention of becoming aware of timing challenges. Processor architects will be directed to the issues of static timing analysis, tool developers can identify key hardware challenges and developers of hard real-time systems will learn about the possibilities and limitations of a static analysis.

The authors would like to thank all the people who contributed to the preparation of this book. Special thanks go to Theo Ungerer, the supervisor of Sascha Uhrig. Moreover, the authors would like to thank all people involved in the research projects referred to throughout the book, all their colleagues and the reviewers who appraised the original habilitation theses.

Christine ROCHANGE
Sascha UHRIG
Pascal SAINRAT
November 2013

1

Real-Time Systems and Time Predictability

This introduction discusses real-time systems and shows how they differ from general purpose computing systems. Different types of real-time systems are explained and examples of these types are given. The need for time predictability of computer systems is exposed and the structure of the book is presented.

1.1. Real-time systems

1.1.1. *Introduction*

Most of the processors in use today are not part of what we usually call *computers*, i.e. servers, workstations, laptops or tablets. They are instead components of hidden computing systems that control and interact with physical environments, also referred to as *embedded systems*. Such systems are developed in a wide range of domains: transport (cars, aircrafts, trains and rockets), household appliances (washing machines and vacuum cleaners), communications (cellular phones, modems and routers), multimedia (MP3 players and set top boxes), construction machinery (drilling machines), production lines (robots), medicine (pacemakers), etc. In cars, for example, embedded software controls the behavior of the engine with the goal of saving fuel and, at the same time, limiting emissions. Digital equipment also provides safety improvement by the means of dedicated functions (e.g. antilock breaking systems and air bags) and the well-being of passengers (e.g. air conditioning, power windows or audio systems). In recent years, the notion of *cyber-physical systems* has been introduced. This refers to such systems that link several computing elements, which tightly interact both among one another and with their physical environment.

Embedded systems typically abide by a number of constraints that go beyond the usual scope of computing systems. Economical considerations, especially for large markets such as those for phones or cars, impose optimizing the cost. This is particularly true for hardware components: even an additional 5 cents is a lot when multiplied by 1,000,000 units. But cost issues also concern software development. For this reason, the reuse of software components (intellectual property (IP) components) is usually favored. Hand-held electronic devices should be as small and as light as possible. But size and, above all, weight may also be an issue in some transportation systems: additional weight usually increases the cost. Mobile devices must exhibit low energy consumption to optimize the life of batteries between charges. Thermal dissipation may be an issue in cases of limited cooling facilities, e.g. in confined spaces. Other constraints are put on systems that operate in harsh environments and are subjected to heat, vibrations, shocks, radio frequency (RF) interference, corrosion water, etc. Components in aerospace systems can be hit by cosmic and high-energy ionizing particles that engender the so-called single event upset that may change the state of bits. Radiation-hardened components are used in spatial systems but also around nuclear reactors.

Furthermore, some embedded systems must fulfill timing constraints: some of the tasks that implement the system must meet deadlines. For such systems, referred to as *real-time systems*, producing results in time is required as much as producing correct results. As a result, part of the system design and verification process consists of performing timing analysis of critical tasks, then checking that they can be scheduled in such a way that they are able to meet their deadlines. Various techniques and tools have been developed for this purpose and will be surveyed throughout this book. In section 1.1.2, the concept of task criticality will be discussed, safety standards will be briefly reviewed in section 1.1.3 and various examples of real-life real-time systems will be discussed in section 1.1.4.

Progress in technology and in computer architecture designs leads to components that offer steadily increasing computing power. Today, increasing clock frequencies in order to obtain higher performance from advanced processors is no longer feasible. So, the trend is to integrate multiple cores on a single chip: the aggregated performance is higher than what can be achieved with single-core architectures, and at the same time the performance/energy ratio is improved. Better performance allows us to consider the implementation of new and advanced functionalities, such as steer-by-wire and brake-by-wire driver-assistance systems, combustion engine control, or automatic emergency-braking tiggered by collision avoidance techniques. These systems can evaluate more sensor signals and master more complex situations if higher performance is provided by future control units. Examples could be online distance measures that trigger higher security actions for passengers such as closing the windows and setting the passenger seats in upright positions if an unavoidable crash is detected. Motor injection could be optimized to reduce gas consumption and emissions through better processor performances. Embedded systems for automotive applications are under permanent pressure of cost, while demanding higher performance due to new standards and Quality-of-Service (QoS). Also of paramount and vital importance is the ability to develop and produce systems that are capable of achieving maximum safety, reliability and availability.

Aerospace applications benefit from more powerful processors by providing support for ever-increasing demands of additional functionality on board or a higher level of comfort through a better control of the actuators and, at the same time, requiring absolute guarantees on the timing performance of the system. In addition, certification requirements (e.g. DO-178C) impose restrictions on proving properties of hardware and software, especially regarding timing. At the very least, a fourfold increase in performance is desired for next-generation aircrafts.

On a similar level, future space applications will require increased performance; however, higher CPU clock frequency rates are not generally feasible due to the increased risk of electromagnetic interference and errors induced from cosmic radiation. In this context, an increase in performance is not due to increasing CPU frequencies, but increasing the number of computation units. The most energy and weight efficient way to achieve this is through multicore processors. Current trends in the development of the freely available LEON family of processors for space applications precisely follow this trend. However, in a project performed for ESA by Rapita Systems called PEAL, it was shown that there are still significant issues regarding the adoption of these advanced features by industry unless provable properties regarding timing can be demonstrated. In aerospace, the demand for reduced weight and size is relentless. Guidance, navigation and control algorithms routinely coexist on a single processor. With the advent of free flight and autonomous flight, we must increasingly co-host many other safety and non-safety critical applications on a common powerful processor to maximally utilize hardware that reduces recurring costs, size, weight and power.

This race for computing performance has consequences on the verification and validation of critical systems. Most schemes implemented in modern processors to achieve high performance exhibit one of the following characteristics: (1) their behavior relies on the execution history (e.g. dynamic branch predictors make their decisions based on the issues of previous branches; cache memories contain instructions and data that have been accessed in the past); (2) their behavior is dynamic, i.e. it depends on information that is only available at runtime (e.g. the way an instruction crosses a pipeline depends on which instructions are in the pipeline at the same time); (3) they speculate on the results of some instructions in order to process other instructions faster. These characteristics combined with a wide range of possible values of input data make the execution profile of tasks difficult to predict at analysis time. With multicore architectures, the sharing of resources (e.g. the interconnection network and part of the memory) among cores adds to the complexity. Paradoxically, a faster architecture does not systematically mean a better chance of meeting deadlines: the sophisticated mechanisms used to increase the instruction rate are often hard, sometimes even impossible, to model, and this may result in longer estimated execution times due to the pessimism engendered by overcautious assumptions. In section 1.2, we review the concept of *time predictability*. One objective of this book is to show why some of the above-mentioned schemes challenge timing analysis techniques   and   to   provide   some   recommendations   for time-predictable architectures. Shortly, the global advice is: *Make the worst case fast and the whole system easy to analyze* [SCH 09b].

1.1.2. *Soft, firm and hard real-time systems*

Real-time systems are commonly divided into the following three categories according to the consequence of missing a deadline (see Figure 1.1):

– In *hard* real-time systems, missing a deadline is a full system failure. Dramatic consequences include environmental disaster, economic crash, or even loss of human lives. An example of such a system is the control unit that triggers inflating air bags during a car crash. The decision to use the air bag is taken from monitoring various sensors, e.g. accelerometers, wheel speed sensors, gyroscopes, seat occupancy sensors and brake pressure sensors. It must be taken in time, i.e. within a given delay after the collision is anticipated, so that the driver and the passengers are protected against hitting the steering wheel and windows. Many other applications in the domain of traveler transportation (e.g. flight control software in an aircraft, signaling systems in trains or antilock braking systems (ABSs) in cars) have strict deadlines. An antimissile system also runs hard real-time tasks: it must destroy any incoming missile before it cause any damage.

– *Firm* real-time systems denote such systems for which a result produced after the deadline is useless and discarded without any catastrophic consequences. It is accepted that some deadlines can be missed if not too frequently. Typical firm real-time systems are encountered in the domain of multimedia applications. In a video conferencing system, audio or video frames that do not reach their destination before their deadline are simply dropped, which may only affect the quality of the received video.

– In *soft* real-time systems, the result produced by a task after its deadline is still useful but the QoS is degraded. Video decoding applications and printer control software belong to this category.

Figure 1.1. *Soft, firm and hard real time*

This book mainly deals with hard real-time systems where it is expected that no failure occurs during the time the system is effective (often referred to as the time of the mission in reference to aeronautics and space systems). Quantitatively, the probability of a hazard occuring, per operational hour, should be less than 10^{-9} [KAS 12]. Achieving such a low probability of failure requires a careful design of the hardware, taking into account the specific constraints of the application domain, the use of fault-tolerance techniques and a normalized process for the development of the software including formal methods to ensure that the system is logically and timely error-prone.

The notion of *criticality* is closely related to the application domain. Transportation systems (airplanes, cars, trains and spacecraft) include critical subsystems for which a failure may translate into injuries to or even death of passengers. This is also true for equipment that may look light at first glance but that requires a high level of reliability, such as amusement park rides. A failure in the control system of a nuclear plant may engender an environmental catastrophe that can also have severe consequences on the health of neighboring people. Some medical devices, such as heart pacemakers, feature safety requirements as well, for obvious reasons. Now, criticality can also be considered through the prism of economical consequences. A failure in an electricity distribution system can put some industries in a difficult situation. A company that produces a component that produces timing errors may suffer economical effects and close if they lose markets.

1.1.3. *Safety standards*

Safety standards exist for several of the application domains mentioned above and their use spreads rapidly [KAS 12]. Their objective is to provide guidelines toward safe software development and validation. Besides guaranteeing the absence of non-functional hazards, they require verifying three points: absence of runtime errors, execution times and memory usage. They define criticality levels and recommend, for each level, a range of techniques and tools to be used to show that the software meets the constraints.

The DO-178C is applicable to aerospace systems. It defines five levels of criticality, from level A (the most critical) to level E (the least critical). The standard promotes software verification through the use of formal techniques, such as abstract interpretation, model checking and theorem proving (it explicitly mentions that dynamic testing "cannot show the absence of errors"). It also recommends model-based software development as well as the use of qualified tools. Worst-case execution time (WCET) is listed as one of the non-functional properties that must be verified. The safety standard for electrical, electronic and programmable electronic systems is the IEC-61508. It considers four safety integrity levels, from SIL1 (the least critical) to SIL4 (the most critical). WCET is also mentioned as a property to be checked and static program analysis is required for levels SIL2–SIL4. The ISO-26262 is for automotive systems and the CENELEC EN-50128 is for railway systems. They both impose analyzing WCETs and response times and recommend static analysis techniques for this purpose. Similar standards exist for medical applications (the EN-60601 and the IEC-62304) and for nuclear plants (IEC-60880).

1.1.4. *Examples*

This section presents several examples of soft and hard real-time systems. Firm real-time systems are not included because of their marginal relevance in practice.

1.1.4.1. *Soft real-time systems*

Soft real-time systems mainly appear in the domain of multimedia and software-defined radio systems. In general, multimedia systems translate a kind of digital data stream into visual or audio signals or vice versa. The visual or audio signals arise from or are consumed by human beings. This is where the real-time constraints come from. The reasons for the real-time constraints are the visual percipiency of human beings and the physical characteristics of audio signals.

1.1.4.1.1. MP3 decoding

The so-called MP3 format for audio data (see [PAN 96]), which was originally called Moving Picture Expert Group (MPEG) layer 3, stores coded data of an audio stream. Several bit resolutions and sample rates are possible as well as the availability of mono- and stereo features.

The audio information stored within an MP3 stream is separated into multiple frames containing 32 or 12 samples, according to the wave band. Depending on the sample rate, each frame correlates to a predefined period of the audio stream. To obtain a proper playback of the MP3 audio stream, these frames must be read, decoded and handed to the output device in time.

Otherwise, a blackout time between the previous frame and the current frame occurs that can be noticed by the listener.

The observed blackout time is a result of a missed deadline, which is provided by the frame length. The execution time of the task that decodes the MP3 stream depends on the data present within the stream and some environmental activities. For example, the user of an MP3 player presses a button on the device while the player is decoding a frame. The pressed button should be handled within a short period of time otherwise the player seems to hang, but the handling could affect the decoding task and thus its execution time.

In the case of this example, a missed deadline results in an unintended blackout but no danger for human beings or machinery can occur. Hence, this example has to be classified as a soft real-time system.

1.1.4.1.2. MPEG decoding

Another example of a soft real-time system is the MPEG video decoding [138 96], which is similar to the MP3 decoding. In contrast to the MP3 coding, the MPEG video streams consist of different kinds of frames. The types of frames have different characteristics with respect to their complexity. The main types are the I, the P and the B frames. The I-type frames contain a whole picture with the full resolution of the video, whereas the two other types are composed of relative pictures, i.e. only deltas are stored within these frames.

During playback, a typical series of frames is I, B, B, P, B, B, I where the P is a delta with respect to the first I and the B frames are related to the preceding I and synchronously to the succeeding P frame and vice versa, respectively. As a result, the P frame has to be decoded before the second frame can be shown. To allow for this circumstance, the frames are stored in a different order within the data stream, e.g. I, P, B, B, I, B, B. Hence, it is required to decode two frames, the P and the first B, to display the second picture (after the initial I frame). Accordingly, it is not required to decode any frame to display the fourth picture, which is the already-decoded P frame.

Because of the different kinds of frames and the way they are decoded, the execution times for decoding the frames strongly depend on the type and the input data and vary extremely. An authentic WCET analysis as described in section 2.2 is nearly impossible and missed deadlines cannot be excluded. The results can be realized in terms of incompletely decoded frames or unsteady movements in the video. Burchard *et. al.* [BUR 99] presented an alternative decoding approach using a predecoding phase as well as precalculated execution times per frame that would be stored inside the stream.

The deadlines for decoding the frames arise from the frame rate used for coding the video stream. If a deadline were missed, it is possible that the succeeding frame or multiple frames would have to be skipped. The reason is that in most cases a video stream is correlated with an audio stream, which is decoded separately. Hence, both streams must proceed synchronously and as a result some video frames have to be skipped if the video decoding is too slow. With respect to the frame skipping, the video decoding can also be regarded as a firm real-time system because late decoded frames are of no use.

1.1.4.1.3. Cell phone audio transmission

Digital telecommunication audio transmission between cell phones consists of many tasks that fulfill the mission of transmitting an audio stream from one human being to another one by a digital signal stream. Figure 1.2 shows an abstract and simplified presentation of the required transmission tasks.

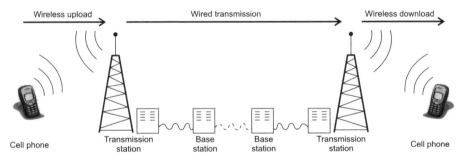

Figure 1.2. *Simplified task chain of an audio telecommunication transmission*

The five tasks, namely *sampling*, *wirelessupload*, *wiredtransmission*, *wirelessdownload* and *playback*, have to meet a single common real-time requirement. The transmission delay should not be noticeable by the participants. This requirement is not very strict because it is a subjective demand.

But, the challenge of telecommunication is to synchronize the required tasks in a way that all data reach the receiver in time. Hence, the sampling cell phone has to meet deadlines to achieve a predefined sampling rate; the wireless upload as well as the wired transmission and the download must guarantee a certain data rate. The last element of the chain has to decode the received stream also using the predefined sampling rate.

The telecommunication sector itself represents a soft real-time system but because of the diversity of participating devices, companies and transport medias, it is a very complex area with respect to the real-time requirements.

1.1.4.2. *Hard real-time systems*

The examples presented in section 1.1.4.1 illustrate some systems with soft real-time requirements. In contrast to these systems, the examples shown in this section can bring danger to human beings or machinery in cases of a missed deadline. Hence, these examples have to be classified as hard real-time systems.

1.1.4.2.1. The air bag system

The air bag should reduce the risk of injury to passengers within a car in case of a crash. Therefore, the air bag control system evaluates the data received from multiple crash sensors. The front air bags must be released in the event of a front crash but they must not be triggered if the crash is from behind or from either side. In addition, at least two crash sensors must report a crash to eliminate fail functions caused by a defect of a crash sensor.

Different types of crash sensors are available: accelerometers detect a high acceleration, pressure sensors measure fast changes of the air pressure within the doors of a car and the so-called Crash Impact Sound Sensing (CISS) systems recognize the sound of deforming metal.

Signals of all these sensors are evaluated by an air bag control unit, which decides if an air bag must be triggered or not. Because the active period of an open air bag is only about 100 ms, the activation of it must be timed very well so that its efficiency is at the maximum. Besides the original velocity of the car, it is also important whether or not the passenger has used his/her seat belt at the time of the crash.

An additional timing constraint originates from other air bags: the opening of an air bag is about 160 decibels loud and brings the risk of acute hearing loss. To minimize this risk, the two front air bags must not be activated at the same time and hence, the air bag of the co-driver is triggered slightly after the driver's air bag.

As real-time constraints of an air bag control system, a simple deadline is not sufficient. Moreover, an exact point of time is required at which the air bag must be triggered. In addition, calculating the point of time on the fly and in time leads to another hard deadline. Missing this deadline or activating the air bag at the wrong time could lead to inadmissible danger for the passengers. In this case, no air bag might be the better solution.

1.1.4.2.2. The antilock braking system

The aim of an ABS in cars and aircrafts is to take care of the grip during extreme braking. Therefore, it tries to avoid the locking of wheels and to sustain static friction, which must not change to dynamic friction. Otherwise, the adhesive force is reduced and the efficiency of the brakes is affected. In addition, preventing the wheels from locking keeps the steering active and the driver or pilot is enabled to control the car or aircraft during hard or emergency braking.

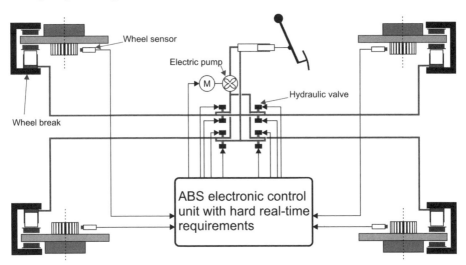

Figure 1.3. *Schematic of an ABS sensor and actuator system*

Figure 1.3 shows a schematic picture of the ABS of a passenger car. The control unit measures the rotation of each wheel independently, mostly by sensors using the so-called Hall effect [POP 04]. These sensors measure the spinning of the wheel more than 50 times per rotation. If a wheel tends to get much slower than the others, the ABS control unit first opens an electromagnetic valve in the hydraulic braking system to reduce the pressure at the particular brake. In a second step, an additional pump is activated, which further reduces the pressure at the brake in order to release it. As a result, the wheel starts spinning again and the valve is closed once again to increase the compression.

Both procedures, opening the valve and closing it, have hard real-time constraints. If the control unit recognizes the locking of a wheel late, the braking effect of this wheel is reduced. Furthermore, if the system misses the time when the wheel properly spins, no braking is available because the valve is still open. Both scenarios could lead to horrible disasters and thus the ABS must be classified as a hard real-time system. Moreover, it is also a safety-critical system but these systems are out of the scope of this work.

1.1.4.2.3. Combustion engine control

Modern combustion engines are managed by a digital control unit, the so-called engine control unit. This unit is responsible for coordinating the ignition, the injection of fuel, the valve timing, the incoming air mass, the exhaust gas recirculation and so on. The main objective of using this electronic unit instead of mechanical motor management, as was used several years ago, is to reduce fuel consumption and environmental pollution. In contrast to the ABS and the air bag system, an engine control unit is not required to improve the safety of the passengers of the car. Nevertheless, if it is applied, it has to be classified as a hard real-time system, which is also safety related. The reason is, for example, that if the ignition is not correctly timed, the rotation speed of the crankshaft could become out of control and, in turn, the speed of the car would be out of control.

The mission of controlling the engine consists of several hard real-time tasks with different timing constraints. Some tasks such as the ignition control depends on the current angle of the crankshaft and some other tasks are related to timing periods. For example, the ignition must be activated several degrees before the corresponding piston reaches its upper dead center. Other tasks such as the exhaust gas recirculation must be managed periodically, independent of the crankshaft.

1.1.4.2.4. Aircraft autopilot

Autopilots for aircraft are very complex systems, starting from multiple systems to control roll, pitch, yaw and throttle, and extend to a redundant system with, for example, three complete autopilots as required for airliners. The autopilot is an inherent part of an airliner and it is active during about 95% of a flight.

Besides the single stand-alone task of each autopilot subsystem, the tasks are related to each other by physicality. For example, during the flight the amount of fuel inside the tanks is reduced, which leads to a lower weight of the aircraft. Hence, to prevent the aircraft from climbing steadily, the pitch control reduces the pitch permanently to stay on a predefined flight level. Because of the lower pitch, the aerodynamic resistance decreases and the aircraft accelerates, which in turn increases the lift again. At this time, the throttle control has to reduce the speed to an optimal speed otherwise an overspeed situation can destroy the aircraft (see Figure 1.4).

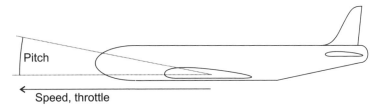

Figure 1.4. *Pitch and throttle of an aircraft*

In order to deal with these physical correlations, all the different tasks of an autopilot have to react to the current situation in time. In addition, the reactions of the tasks have to be coordinated and scheduled in order to prevent an oscillating situation where one task counteracts the actions of other tasks or the actions of two tasks accumulate. This could happen in the previous example if pitch control further reduces the pitch to prevent further climbing, while the throttle also decreases speed.

1.1.4.2.5. Hydraulic motor control

An example without any direct impact on human life but on the functionality of a piece of technical machinery is the control logic of hydraulic motors. To increase the torque of the drill shown in Figure 1.5, two hydraulic motors are used in parallel. These two motors have to be activated simultaneously to avoid damages. Because the motors are coupled physically, starting one motor before the other motor would force the second motor to rotate without oil flow. As a result, a low pressure inside it leads to a vacuum, which is explosively filled up by the following high pressure when the second motor is started. The problem is that this event could lead to a delamination of swarf, which can damage the hydraulic pump at a later point of time.

Two hydraulic motors
to reach the required torque

Figure 1.5. *Drilling machine with two hydraulic motors*

Of course, this seems to be a very simple real-time system compared to an autopilot because it is only required to open two valves simultaneously. But, if these valves are controlled by two different control units, a communication delay must be taken into account. In addition, this real-time scenario can be found inside an aircraft multiple times. Because of redundancy reasons, most rudders are moved by two hydraulic cylinders that are supplied by two hydraulic circuits and controlled by different control units. Hence, the problem of opening multiple valves simultaneously is also present as a small real-time task inside a very complex real-time environment.

1.2. Time predictability

Most of the computing systems exhibit high-performance requirements and the achieved performance of hardware and software is generally measured on the *average* case, i.e. on some executions that are considered as representative of most of the executions.

In hard real-time systems, aside from performance requirements, is the need for being able to show that real-time tasks can always meet their deadlines. For this purpose, the WCETs of critical tasks must be determined. This is possible only if the hardware architecture is time-predictable or time-analyzable. These two expressions are often used without distinction. However, Grund *et al.* [GRU 11b] formalize these concepts. They show that predictability (i.e. the ability to be predicted) is generally not a Boolean property, but can instead be expressed by a range of levels that allow comparing two systems ("A is more predictable than B"). Predictability can be seen as the ability to take into account a hardware scheme with a certain level of accuracy. The maximal accuracy is reached when the behavior of the system can be exactly predicted. Instead, analyzability is related to the approach used for timing analysis. It indicates the capacity of this approach to predict a given property.

A key point is that a real-time system does not necessarily have to exhibit high performance. Conversely, a high-performance processor may not fit the requirements of real-time systems. A common pitfall is to believe that a solution for making sure that a critical task will meet its deadline is to run it on a fast processor. Unfortunately, if the average execution time is usually improved by using a faster processor, this may not be the case for the WCET due to predictability/analyzability issues. The complexity of some of the schemes used to achieve high performance often makes the timing analysis complex and pessimistic. As a result, the WCET computed considering a high-performance processor may be longer than that obtained considering a simpler processor. In addition, the variability of execution times is generally higher when the processor implements sophisticated mechanisms and the observed execution time might be far from the estimated WCET, which may be a problem.

1.3. Book outline

The purpose of this book is threefold: (1) to offer an overview of the state-of-the-art techniques in the field of timing analysis of hard real-time systems, (2) to provide an insight into the difficulties raised by advanced architectural schemes with respect to such timing analysis and (3) to review existing techniques toward the design of time-predictable processors.

Chapter 2 provides background information on timing analysis approaches. First, an overview of task scheduling techniques, both for single-score and multicore systems, is given. These techniques all consider estimations of the WCET of tasks, i.e. their maximum possible execution time, whatever the input data values and the initial state of the hardware platform. Various approaches can be used to determine WCET estimates: some of them rely on measurements of the program execution on the target hardware, while other approaches consider models of the hardware as part of static program analyses. The main lines of such approaches are reviewed. The chapter ends with a discussion on the notion of time composability.

Chapter 3 focuses on current processor architectures. It studies the main schemes implemented in the execution core to enhance the average-case performance: pipelining, superscalar execution, multithreading and branch prediction. Each of them is first presented, and then state-of-the-art techniques to determine their worst-case timing behavior are introduced. Finally, directions to improve its timing predictability are discussed.

Chapter 4 deals with the memory hierarchy: instruction and data caches, scratchpad memories and the external main memory. The specificities of each level of the hierarchy are reviewed. Then, the basic existing approaches to analyze the worst-case behavior of such memories are presented and recommendations to build time-predictable memory systems are given.

Chapter 5 deals with multicore architectures that are now unavoidable when designing high-performance embedded systems. Multicore architectures are beneficial in terms of integration and power efficiency from the sharing of resources among cores. However, this sharing challenges the timing analysis of critical software because individual tasks can no longer be analyzed separately. At the same time, the global analysis of several concurrent tasks jointly does not seem feasible: first, this raises computational complexity issues and second, the set of tasks that run concurrently is often decided dynamically. For these reasons, it is necessary to consider specific schemes to control resource sharing to some extent, in order to favor timing composability. This allows the use of timing analysis techniques that are close to those developed for single-core architectures. In this chapter, we review such hardware schemes.

Finally, Chapter 6 describes single-core and multicore architectures that have been designed in several academic and European projects, with time predictability as a main objective. These architectures may inspire future commercial designs once the view to time predictability spreads over application domains that require time-critical software design.

2

Timing Analysis of Real-Time Systems

As seen in Chapter 1, a real-time system usually includes a set of tasks that are activated in response to some events (e.g. an interruption triggered by a timer or an input device). Some of these tasks exhibit timing constraints: in this book, we focus on hard real-time systems where tasks *must* absolutely meet their deadlines. When the number of computing resources (e.g. the number of processing cores) is lower than the number of tasks that can be simultaneously active, the way a given resource is successively allocated to different tasks should guarantee that all their timing constraints can be fulfilled. This is what *real-time task scheduling* deals with. In this chapter, we will first give an overview of task scheduling strategies. Then, we will focus on techniques to determine the *worst-case execution time* (WCET) of a real-time task. A good knowledge of the challenges in this domain is key to understanding time-predictability issues when designing architectural support for time-critical systems.

2.1. Real-time task scheduling

2.1.1. *Task model*

Real-time task scheduling provides answers for two questions: (1) can all the tasks in the system fulfill their timing constraints? (2) if so, how can they do it, i.e. how should resources (processing cores first of all) be allocated so that all deadlines can be met?

Solutions to these issues consider task properties, as those defined in Liu's model for periodic tasks [LIU 73]:

– The *release time* (i) is the time at which a new task occurrence (a *job*) is ready for being scheduled.

– The *deadline* (D) is the time by which the job should be terminated, after it has been released.

– The *WCET* (C) of the task is its longest possible execution time, whatever the input values and the execution context.

– The period of the task (T) is the interval between two successive activations of the task.

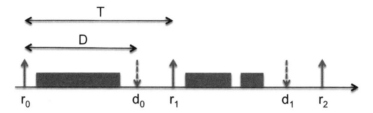

Figure 2.1. *A periodic real-time task*

Periodic tasks are activated at fixed rate, e.g. as part of a control loop. Many scheduling algorithms are targeted to such periodic tasks. However, real-time systems may also include sporadic and aperiodic tasks. An aperiodic task has irregular arrival times. A sporadic task is also activated irregularly but its minimum arrival interval is known.

2.1.2. *Objectives of task scheduling algorithms*

The main goal of a scheduling algorithm is to guarantee that all the hard real-time tasks can meet their deadlines. To reach this goal, a valid task schedule is computed *offline* or *online*. Offline scheduling precomputes the schedule of tasks and stores it in a table that is used by a sequencer at runtime. This avoids overloading the processor by the execution of a scheduling algorithm and this approach is usually preferred in highly critical systems. An online scheduler takes scheduling decisions at runtime, e.g. on each arrival of a task. This approach is more flexible, particularly in the presence of sporadic tasks. For safety, the feasibility of scheduling should be initially assessed. In the best-case scenario, when (necessary and) sufficient conditions related to the scheduling strategy are fulfilled, schedulability can be checked through analytical computations that are feasible in polynomial time. Otherwise, checking the schedulability is an NP-hard problem [LEU 82]. Simulating the application in a bounded time window can be a solution.

Another objective of a scheduling algorithm may be to optimize the utilization of resources, e.g. the processing core. The utilization of the processor by the set of n tasks of an application is given by:

$$U = \sum_{i=1}^{n} \frac{C_i}{P_i}$$

A necessary condition for the system to be schedulable is: $U \leq 1$.

Task scheduling can be preemptive or not. To favor time predictability, cooperative strategies can also be considered: tasks can be preempted at predefined points in their code. Reducing the number of context switches (and then their cost) may be another target of a task scheduling algorithm.

For some classes of applications, some algorithms are considered *optimal*. An algorithm is optimal in its category for a class of applications if and only if, for any application in this class, (1) it can be scheduled by the algorithm, or (2) no other algorithm in the same category can schedule it.

2.1.3. *Mono-processor scheduling for periodic tasks*

2.1.3.1. *Offline scheduling*

Offline scheduling generates a static task schedule that is then enforced without any change at runtime. In addition to time constraints, it can consider precedence relations among tasks as well as sharing of resources. As it has a full view of the task set, it can optimize (reduce) the number of context switches due to task preemption.

Offline scheduling is often supposed to provide better guarantees than dynamic schemes since the schedules can be checked prior to the execution of the system. The overhead time needed to schedule tasks at runtime is also reduced to minimum. However, any change to the system may require recomputing the whole schedule, which may be prohibitive when the system changes frequently. In addition, static scheduling cannot handle aperiodic tasks in an optimized way.

2.1.3.2. *Fixed-priority scheduling*

For this category of algorithms, the priorities of the tasks are decided offline and do no change during execution. This reduces the cost of dynamic scheduling.

The *rate monotonic* (RM) algorithm assigns priorities that are inversely proportional to the task periods [LIU 73]. This algorithm is optimal (among fixed-priority algorithms) for sets of independent periodic tasks that have deadlines equal to their periods and that are all released simultaneously. For such sets of n tasks, a sufficient condition for schedulability with RM is:

$$U \leq n(2^{\frac{1}{n}} - 1)$$

The *deadline monotonic* (DM) strategy considers tasks that may have their deadlines earlier than their periods: they are assigned priorities that are inversely proportional to their deadlines [LEU 82]. This algorithm is optimal among fixed-priority schemes for applications consisting of independent tasks released simultaneously. A sufficient condition for schedulability with DM is:

$$\sum_{i=1}^{n} \frac{C_i}{D_i} \leq n(2^{\frac{1}{n}} - 1)$$

2.1.3.3. *Dynamic-priority scheduling*

Dynamic-priority scheduling algorithms recompute the task priorities each time a new task occurrence is released. This increases the cost of runtime scheduling but generally improves the schedulability of applications.

The *earliest deadline first* (EDF) scheme gives the highest priority to the task that has the nearest deadline [LIU 73, STA 98]. It has been shown to be optimal for sets of independent periodic tasks [DER 74]. A necessary and sufficient condition for a system of n independent periodic tasks that have their deadlines equal to their periods is: $U \leq 1$ [COF 76].

The *least laxity* (LL) algorithm considers the task laxities [DER 89]. The laxity of a task occurrence is defined as the difference between its deadline and its remaining workload. On a mono-processor platform, LL generates a larger number of preemptions than EDF.

2.1.4. *Scheduling sporadic and aperiodic tasks*

Two classes of approaches may be considered to schedule aperiodic tasks together with periodic tasks: the first class consists of stealing idle CPU cycles (i.e. cycles not executing a periodic task); the second class defines a fictitious periodic task that serves aperiodic tasks and is scheduled as any other periodic task.

A *background server* schedules aperiodic tasks in idle processor cycles. It is simple to implement and does not impair the schedulability of periodic tasks (any scheduling algorithm can be considered for them). However, if the periodic load is high, background service opportunities may be very few and the response times of aperiodic tasks increase. More complex strategies modify the scheduling of periodic tasks to improve the response time of aperiodic tasks. The *slack stealing* algorithm defers periodic tasks (keeping the guarantee that they will meet their deadlines) to schedule aperiodic tasks as soon as possible [THU 94].

A *polling server* is implemented as a periodic task. At each activation, it executes pending aperiodic tasks (if any) during its reserved execution time. An aperiodic task that is released just after the polling server task ends may have a poor response time. A *deferrable server* dynamically extends the execution time of the server tasks as needed to serve pending aperiodic tasks until the point where periodic tasks must absolutely be scheduled to meet their deadlines. Both these servers are designed to run under the RM scheduling algorithm. Other servers fit dynamic-priority scheduling algorithms, like EDF. The *dynamic priority exchange server* exchanges its runtime with lower priority (periodic) tasks when no aperiodic task is pending. This time can be retrieved later when an aperiodic task is released [SPU 96].

2.1.5. *Multiprocessor scheduling for periodic tasks*

Multiprocessor scheduling has two targets: (1) allocating the tasks to the processing cores; and (2) deciding in which order task instances should execute. In [CAR 04], a two-dimension taxonomy of multiprocessor scheduling strategies is proposed.

First, a *migration-based* classification distinguishes between schemes that (1) do not allow task migration (this is also called *partitioned scheduling*); (2) allow task-level migration (an instance of a task cannot migrate, but successive instances of a task may run on different cores); (3) consider job-level migration (a task instance can migrate; this strategy is known as *global scheduling*). Second, a *priority-based* classification considers three ways of handling priorities: (1) fixed for a task (all its instances have the same priority), (2) fixed for a task instance and (3) dynamic.

A larger survey on real-time scheduling for multiprocessors is given in [DAV 11].

2.2. Task-level analysis

The execution time of an application generally depends on the initial state of the hardware. For example, it can be influenced by the instructions that are in progress in the pipeline when the task starts. Similarly, the contents of the instruction/data caches impact the latency of instruction/data fetches. More globally, the effects of the initial hardware state on the execution time processors are due to advanced schemes implemented in modern processors: their behavior is strongly related to the execution history.

The execution time of a task is also determined by the execution path, which is governed by the values of inputs, through conditional branches. Often, a large number of inputs together with wide value ranges generate a huge number of possible paths, then a huge number of possible execution time values. Figure 2.2 shows the probabilities of various execution time values for an example task. *Assuming that the task could be run with each possible input data set and any possible initial hardware state*, the number of possible executions is denoted by N, and the number of times the execution time equals e is denoted by $n[e]$. Each bar on the graph reflects a probability $n[e]/N$. The longest execution time observed in this context, E, is the real WCET (r-WCET) of the task. Usually, it is not possible to observe all the possible executions of a task. Instead, a timing analysis determines an upper bound of the r-WCET, referred to as *estimated* WCET (e-WCET, or WCET for short).

Determining the WCET of tasks makes it possible to check that their deadlines can be met (1) by dimensioning the hardware platform so that the

WCETs are compatible with the deadlines, and (2) by enabling the computation of a valid task schedule. In the following, we review existing WCET analysis techniques.

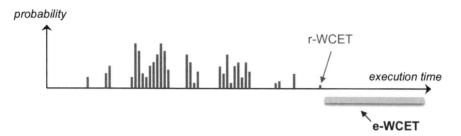

Figure 2.2. *Execution time distribution*

Determining the WCET of a program consists of (1) identifying all the possible execution paths, (2) computing the execution times of all the possible paths, or at least of a set of paths that can be guaranteed to include the longest path and (3) determining the longest possible execution time. In practice, identifying the possible execution paths consists of computing loop bounds and of excluding infeasible paths. Loop bounds are absolutely required, unless it is not possible to upper bound the execution time. Additional information on conditional statements (e.g. "this branch is taken every second time") contributes to refining WCET estimates. Execution times depend on the target hardware architecture and its features and parameters must be taken into account.

To perform these three steps, two kinds of approaches can be considered: either real executions of the software on the real target hardware or on a cycle-level simulator can be observed; or static analysis based on representations of the hardware and of the program code is developed. This is explained further in the following sections.

2.2.1. *Flow analysis: identifying possible paths*

2.2.1.1. *Measurement-based flow analysis*

To observe the behavior of an application along all its possible paths, a straightforward approach would consist of generating all the possible input data sets, which is generally infeasible when the number of inputs is large and when the range of their possible values is wide. The time needed to perform all the measurements would be prohibitive. Another solution is to determine input data sets that cover all the possible paths. This is the objective of the PathCrawler tool [WIL 09] that instruments the code to collect a symbolic execution trace with a randomly chosen input data set. From this trace, a path predicate is built and used to exclude all the input data sets that control the same path before selecting another input data set. The operation is repeated until all the possible paths have been tested. But the exhaustive exploration of the possible paths can still be very costly. Lundqvist [LUN 99a] has proposed a different approach based on the use of a cycle-level simulator. Their idea is the following: all the input data are first labeled as *unknown* and these values are propagated through the computations by the simulator (e.g. an addition that has an unknown operand gives an unknown result, but a logical AND with an unknown operand and a null operand gives a null result). When a conditional branch with an unknown condition is encountered, both branches are explored. The complete simulation time may be long.

2.2.1.2. *Static flow analysis*

Flow analysis first consists of building a representation of the program. It may be a syntax tree that reflects the structure of the source code. But some compiler optimizations make it difficult to strictly relate a node or a leaf of the syntax tree to a sequence of instructions. Thus, a control flow graph (CFG) is usually preferred since it expresses the structure of the executable code on which the timing analysis should be based. Building the CFG from the executable code is a quite an easy task [COO 02], except when the program includes indirect branches, whose target is computed at runtime. Value analysis techniques, as the one proposed in [CAS 13], help in predicting those targets at analysis time.

Another side of flow analysis is determining the so-called *flow facts* like loop bounds, or the frequency of some conditional branches. Determining flow facts can be very basic (information is required from the user by the means of annotations [KIR 07]) or automated: many research results have been published in this domain [ALT 96b, HEA 00, CUL 07, ERM 07, HOL 07, DE 08]. Automated analysis can be performed on the source code, which exhibits the program semantics, or on the binary code [STE 07]: this is especially useful when the program under analysis contains calls to library functions seen as black boxes (their source code is not available).

In [ASA 13], existing techniques to extract, express and exploit the program semantics along the model-based development workflow are given an overview.

We will see later in this chapter how these flow facts can be exploited to compute WCETs.

2.2.2. *Low-level analysis: determining partial execution times*

2.2.2.1. *Measurement-based low-level analysis*

The main advantage of referring to measurements done on the real hardware is that no modeling of the architecture is required, which avoids errors (even if interpreting hardware counters may not be straightforward). However, measurements require a testing infrastructure that may be costly to set up. Moreover, it may be difficult to control the initial state of the hardware (which has an impact on the observed execution times). Finally, these techniques require the target hardware to be available at analysis time, which may not be achieved in early phases of a project.

Using a simulator removes some of the difficulties mentioned above: the simulator can be developed ahead of the hardware and setting up software probes is usually easy when the source code of the simulator is available. However, developing a simulator is a hard task and is prone to errors (either coding errors or approximations due to the lack of details on the architecture in the user manual).

Execution times can be observed either on complete execution paths, or on partial paths. Observing complete paths does not allow determining the WCET unless all the possible paths are explored since the longest path may be missed. Despite that, it is still a widespread approach in industrial projects (except for those that must undergo strict certification procedures, like in the avionics domain). Considering safety margins, which are empirically chosen, is not sufficient to achieve a high level of reliability. Moreover, wider safety margins may lead to underusing the hardware, which is not harmless in a context where costs and energy consumption are to be minimized.

Measuring partial paths may, however, be useful to support WCET analysis. Often, partial paths consist of basic blocks[1] or short sequences of basic blocks. Their individual execution times can later be combined to produce the whole WCET of the application. The RapiTime tool [RAP 09] is based on such techniques. It instruments the source code by inserting the so-called *Ipoints* [BET 10] that are expanded as labels in the executable code. At runtime, a timestamped trace is collected and used to determine execution times between pairs of successive Ipoints. However, when the target processor exhibits an history-dependent behavior (which is the case for most of the processors, due to mechanisms such as the pipeline, cache memories and branch predictors), the execution time measured for one basic block may not be its WCET.

Approaches such as single-path programming [PUS 03] increase the interest for measurement-based techniques. The idea is to remove conditional branches and instead to favor conditional (predicated) instructions. In this way, the program has a single path, which can be directly measured to get the single value of the execution time. However, predicated codes generally achieve smaller performance than traditional codes with conditional branches.

2.2.2.2. *Static low-level analysis*

The so-called low-level analysis determines the execution times of code units (basic blocks), considering a model of the target hardware. All the mechanisms that have an impact on execution times, e.g. the pipeline, the branch predictor (when enabled), instructions and data caches, must be considered. We will detail modeling approaches in Chapter 3.

Computing the execution times of basic blocks (instead of measuring them) is possible only if enough details on the architecture are known to build a realistic model. In practice, the user manuals of processors do not provide such information and remain imprecise on the mechanisms used to control the instruction flow through the pipeline: this is a major source of uncertainty of WCET estimates. Should a detailed specification of the core expressed with an architecture description language (ADL) be available, an approach like that described in [SCH 10] could be used to automatically generate a model from a VHDL description.

---

1 A basic block is a sequence of instructions with a single entry point (its first instruction) and a single exit point (its last instruction).

As we will see in Chapter 3, the execution time of a basic block is not constant and generally depends on the execution history, i.e. on the basic blocks that have been executed before it. They determine the state of the hardware (processor core, memory hierarchy and interconnection infrastructure) when the basic block starts its execution. The state of the lower levels of the memory hierarchy (caches) is also highly dependent on the execution history, since the dynamic execution path that leads to the basic block fetches instructions and loads data. Such mechanisms must be considered as part of a global analysis that takes into account all the possible paths without exploring them all one by one. Techniques such as abstract interpretation [COU 77] are often used. This will be detailed in Chapter 4. At the core level, the state is more *local* and mainly consists of registers and instruction queue states. From the core state, and from the processor model that specifies how instructions are processed, static analysis techniques somewhat *simulate* the execution of the basic block to derive its execution time. Naturally, this local simulation must be performed for each possible initial hardware state of the basic block. Building the set of possible initial states can be done using abstract interpretation techniques [SCH 99]. Alternatively, the analysis of how a basic block executes in the processor can be performed on a parameterized specification of the initial state and its worst-case instance is determined in the same time as the block WCET [ROC 09]. In [LI 06], the theoretical worst-case initial state (which is independent of the program of the analysis and may not appear at runtime) is considered.

2.2.3. *WCET computation*

Once the possible paths (loop bounds, infeasible paths, etc.) have been identified and the WCETs of basic blocks have been determined, the whole program WCET can be computed. Two kinds of program representation can be considered for this task [AHO 07]: syntax trees and CFGs. They are illustrated in Figure 2.3. In a syntax tree, nodes stand for source-code-level control flow statements (loops, conditionals and sequence) and leaves stand for basic blocks. In a CFG, nodes represent basic blocks and edges express the possible control flow.

Tree-based approaches [PUS 89, SHA 89] consider the syntax tree representation. Each basic block is weighted by its WCET. These weights are combined and propagated to compute the execution times of nodes, from the leaves up to the root of the tree. These approaches are simple to implement and fast. However, syntax trees can be built for well-structured codes only [SAL 75], and may not be usable when the compiler alters the code structure (e.g. through optimizations).

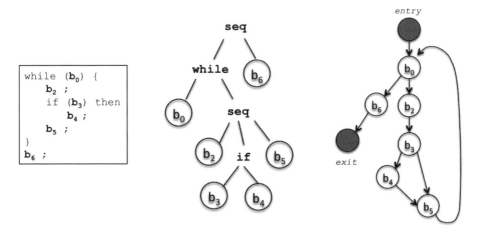

Figure 2.3. *Example program, and its representations as a syntax tree and a control flow graph*

The most popular method works on CFGs. It consists of expressing the global execution time as the weighted sum of the individual basic blocks execution times, where weights represent the basic blocks execution counts. Then, the objective is to maximize this expression of the execution time under a set of constraints that express the results of the former analyses (flow facts and partials WCETs). In this way, an integer linear program (ILP) is built, where variables are the execution counts of basic blocks and of edges. Using a dedicated solving tool (e.g. lp_solve and ILOG CPLEX) allows computing the WCET. The solution is expressed as the maximum execution time value (the WCET) and as the set of variable values, i.e. the set of basic blocks' execution counts. In this way, the longest path is implicitly defined since the order in which the basic blocks are executed is not specified: this explains the name of this method, *implicit path enumeration technique* (IPET) [LI 95a].

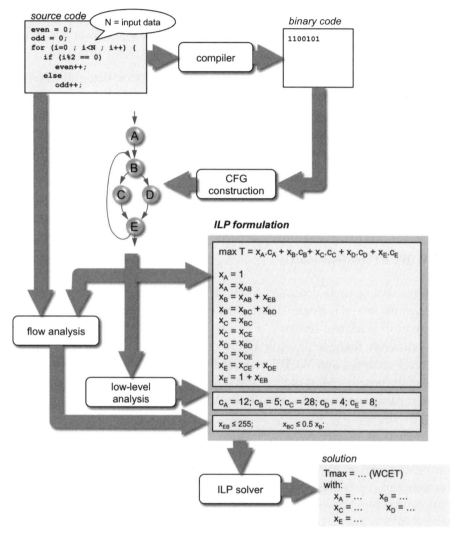

Figure 2.4. *Flow of the IPET method*

This is illustrated in Figure 2.4. The linear program includes:

– an objective function: maximizing the sum of the basic blocks' execution times (c_i) weighted by their execution counts (x_i);

– constraints that express the structure of the CFG (in the style of Kirchhoff's law for electronic circuits): the execution count of one node (x_i) is the sum of the execution counts of its input edges (x_{ji}). It also equals the sum of the execution counts of its output edges (x_{ij}). The entry node is executed once;

– constraints that express the WCETs of basic blocks, determined by the low-level analysis (e.g. $c_A = 12$);

– flow constraints that express the results of flow analysis. In this example, the execution count of the back edge of the loop is upper bounded by 255 times the execution count of the entry edge: this expresses that the loop iterates at most 255 times (this is the loop bound) at each of its executions. Another constraint is put on edge $B \rightarrow C$ to denote that this path is taken every second execution of the loop.

2.2.4. *WCET analysis tools*

A number of tools dedicated to WCET analysis exist: some of them are commercialized (aiT, Bound-T and RapiTime), while others are developed as a support to academic research (Chronos, Heptane, Metamoc, Otawa, Sweet and TuBound). Some tools cover all the steps of WCET analysis (i.e. flow and low-level analysis, and WCET computation), while others focus on specific parts of the process. Most of them use static analysis techniques, but a few rely (at least partly) on measurements. Table 2.1 summarizes the features of current WCET tools.

Reports from the WCET Tool Challenge, in which some of the tools mentioned above have participated, provide insights in their respective features and capabilities [VON 11].

2.2.5. *Alternative approaches to WCET analysis*

2.2.5.1. *Solutions using timed automata and model checking*

Model checking [CLA 86, QUE 82] is a class of techniques used to verify dynamic systems, i.e. to assess that these systems fulfill given properties. It can be used to solve two problems of WCET analysis: (1) predicting the behavior of hardware mechanisms, e.g. cache memories [MET 04, HUB 09, DAL 10] in the low-level analysis phase; and (2) finding the longest path in a CFG, in the final WCET computation phase, instead of, e.g., using the IPET method.

aiT	aiT is a commercial tool by AbsInt[2] that uses static analysis techniques to compute safe WCET upper bounds. It can consider various target processors, including some advanced architectural features such as complex pipelines, caches and branch predictors. The tool provides flow analysis but the user can specify additional flow facts through manual annotations. Graphical visualization of the results is available. aiT is actively used in the avionics, aeronautics and automotive industries, as reported, e.g., in [SOU 05].
Bound-T	Bound-T also uses static analysis techniques. It is commercially distributed by Tidorum Ltd.[3]. It performs advanced flow analysis as well as low-level analysis considering time-predictable microcontrollers.
Chronos	Chronos [LI 07] was developed at the National University of Singapore and implements static analysis approaches. It models various hardware mechanisms that are present in modern processors. It is open source code and is intended to support research work.
Heptane	Heptane is an academic tool from INRIA/University of Rennes. It uses static analysis approaches and focuses on low-level analysis. It supports user-provided flow facts through user annotations.
Metamoc	Metamoc [DAL 10] converts the CFG of a task into a timed automata model that is combined with a model of the target hardware. The UPPAAL model checker is then used to determine the maximum value that a cycle counter can reach, which gives an estimation of the WCET. Flow facts must be provided as user annotations.
Otawa	Otawa [BAL 11] is a toolset dedicated to static WCET analysis designed at University of Toulouse. With its companion tool oRange [DE 08], which focuses on flow analysis, it performs all steps of WCET estimation and implements most of state-of-the-art techniques. It has been designed to be easily retargeted to new platforms.
RapiTime	RapiTime is a commercial tool released by Rapita Systems Ltd.[4]. It implements hybrid measurement-based techniques. The execution times of short code segments are observed at runtime on instrumented code and then combined using static analysis techniques to produce WCET estimates.
Sweet	Sweet (Swedish WCET analysis tool) was developed at Mälardalen Real-Time Research Center. It mainly focuses on flow analysis, using an intermediate format to represent code, named ALF [GUS 09]. It is based on abstract execution techniques [GUS 06] and derives flow constraints from execution counters.
TuBound	TuBound [KNO 12] is a research prototype from Vienna University of Technology that mainly focuses on flow analysis.

Table 2.1. *Commercial and academic WCET tools*

---

2 www.absint.com

3 www.bound-t.com

4 http://www.rapitasystems.com/

The CFG of the program under analysis is translated into a timed automaton [MET 04]. A sequence of states in this automaton represents a concrete (possible) path in the program. To determine the WCET of a program, a model checker can be used to prove the following property: *the execution time of a path in the control flow graph cannot exceed N cycles* [MET 04]. Starting from an initial estimation of the WCET (that may have been obtained by measurements or by any rough analysis), a binary search is performed as follows: if the proof of the property by the model checker fails, then N is increased for the next step; otherwise, it is decreased. The process may be stopped when the difference between the highest value of N for which the proof fails and the lowest value of N for which it succeeds is lower than a given threshold.

The strength of model checking approaches is that they consider concrete paths and then avoid the overestimation of ILP-based solutions due to considering abstract paths. On the other hand, model checking generates very long analysis times and may not be able to handle large applications and complex hardware schemes.

2.2.5.2. *Evolutionary testing*

Evolutionary approaches have been investigated as a way of determining an input data set that produces the WCET of a program. In [WEG 98], an initial random population of data sets is processed by an evolutionary algorithm that aims at increasing the execution time (this includes selection, recombination, mutation and reinsertion operations). Such solutions can be used when the WCET estimation does not need to be safe, either as a stand-alone technique or to compute relevant data sets for hybrid (static/dynamic) WCET analysis.

2.2.5.3. *Probabilistic approaches*

The notion of a probabilistic hard real-time system was introduced in [BER 02]. It denotes a system that must be proved to meet timing constraints *with a high probability*. The authors also define the concept of execution profiles to describe the probabilistic timing behavior of the code section. Execution profiles are combined along the CFG of the program under analysis, using appropriate operators. The result is an end-to-end execution time profile that describes the probabilistic distribution of the execution time.

The motivation for the PROARTIS European project [CAZ 13] comes from the following observation: the complexity of static WCET analysis techniques is mainly due to the necessity of building an as-precise-as-possible view of the impact of the execution history on the hardware state at each point of the program. Any (over-) approximation of this impact may degrade the accuracy of the WCET estimation. To overcome the complexity of accounting for the execution history, the proposed approach randomizes the timing behavior of hardware and software components. This results in a smooth distribution of the execution time probabilities. Then, a WCET probability distribution is computed using techniques based on extreme value theory (EVT). Larger possible values exhibit a very low probability of occurrence. The lowest value for which the cumulative probability is above the desired level of confidence is considered as the WCET estimation. Figure 2.5 illustrates the approach.

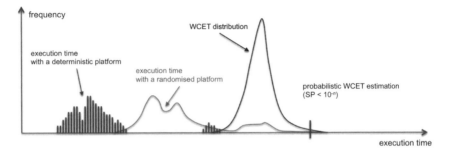

Figure 2.5. *Distribution of execution times on a deterministic versus randomized platform [CAZ 13]*

Two kinds of analysis are considered in PROARTIS. For the *static probabilistic timing analysis*, a model of the hardware is used to determine execution time probability distributions for individual operations. For the *measurement-based probabilistic timing analysis*, the program is run on the target (randomized) hardware to collect timing information. The main challenge for the applicability of these approaches is the availability of such randomized platforms.

2.2.6. *Time composability*

In the following chapters, we will give an overview of existing techniques for modeling the behavior of the various schemes found in current processors.

Most of these techniques focus on a single scheme, and yet require a significant amount of computation and temporary memory storage. Considering several schemes together, combining the associated analysis techniques, exacerbates complexity. For this reason, it is desirable to be able to achieve *time composability*, i.e. to be able to analyze the behavior of the various components independently and then to combine their respective effects on the program timing. For example, the WCET analysis is simplified if (1) any instruction fetch or data load is considered as a cache hit when computing the WCETs of basic blocks, and (2) the global worst-case number of cache misses, weighted by the cache miss penalty, is added later to the program WCET. Unfortunately, we will see that this may be unsafe for modern processors.

Time composability also means that the WCET of a task (thread) can be computed independently from that of other tasks (threads). The reason why the WCET of a task would depend on the behavior of co-running tasks is the sharing of resources, e.g. in multithread processors or in multicore architectures. Sharing may result in conflicts and then engender delays for some tasks. Accounting for such delays may be delicate when the control (arbitration) of resource sharing makes decisions dynamically, i.e. as a function of the respective behavior of tasks. In that case, the tasks must be analyzed conjunctly, which may rapidly become tricky. An example of such analysis is described in [CRO 03] where the WCET of concurrent threads in a network processor is computed, based on a combination of the thread CFGs. Another reason why the WCET of a task should not depend on concurrent tasks is that those concurrent tasks might not be known at analysis time. This can happen when several independent applications share the same hardware platforms, e.g. as in integrated modular avionics (IMA) approaches. This can also be the case when tasks are scheduled dynamically.

In this book, we focus on the time composability related to the hardware platform. But this concept is also applicable to operating systems [BAL 12] and to application-level software [SIF 01, FRE 07]. It can also be considered in the analysis process, through the formal combination of the results of partial analyses [BAL 09, DE 10].

3

Current Processor Architectures

Modern processor architectures implement advanced hardware schemes to accelerate the execution of instructions: pipelining, out-of-order execution, branch prediction, speculative execution. All of them challenge the timing analysis of code snippets, such as basic blocks. In this chapter, we review these schemes, show how they can be analyzed and provide some recommendations for timing predictability.

3.1. Pipelining

Current processors are mostly implemented in a pipelined fashion. In contrast to a non-pipeline processor, where all steps of instruction execution are performed one after another, a pipelined processor executes several steps of the execution of different instructions in parallel. A more detailed description of a pipelined processor is presented by Hennessy and Patterson [HEN 07]. They describe a simple pipeline with four stages. For a better understanding of the pipeline effects that arise in modern processors, the following sections focus on a longer pipeline structure.

Figure 3.1 shows a rough block diagram of the basic stages of a pipelined processor with six pipeline stages. The first stage (instruction fetch stage) is responsible for fetching instructions out of some kind of memory and delivering them to the following pipeline stage. The second stage is called decode stage, because it determines the kind of the instruction, the instruction format, the operands and the operation itself. The required operands are read from the register file in the third pipeline stage and the operation is performed in the fourth stage. If a memory access is required, the following stage is responsible for hiding the memory latency. The last pipeline stage (write back) writes the result of the operation or the value read from the memory back into the register file. Because of the two stages in between reading from the register file and writing to it, a so-called forwarding technique is applied that allows registers to be read from the operand fetch stage before they are written by the write-back stage.

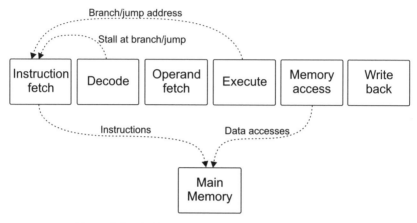

Figure 3.1. *Block diagram of a basic six-stage pipeline*

Depending on the actual implementation of the pipeline, several stages can be merged together or further split into multiple stages. Increasing the number of pipeline stages allows a higher pipeline frequency with the drawback of longer latencies and some worst-case execution time (WCET) problems as described in the following sections.

3.1.1. *Pipeline effects*

In contrast to non-pipelined processors, pipelines can increase the execution speed dramatically, because theoretically it is possible to finish the execution of one instruction at each cycle. Unfortunately, several instructions such as branches and memory load accesses require multiple cycles leading to a delay and a performance reduction. The reasons for these delays are different:

Branches: instructions are fetched at the first pipeline stage. Unfortunately, the outcome of a conditional branch and the target address of an indirect jump are known only near the end of the pipeline. Hence, the fetch stage has to stall until the next instruction is determined. Moreover, the fact that the currently fetched instruction is a branch or a conditional jump is not known by the fetch stage (but only by the decode stage), which does not allow the fetch stage to stall immediately. In fact, the fetch stage triggers at least one more subsequent fetch before it is stalled by the decode stage. In the case of an instruction cache being used, this additional fetch may unnecessarily evict a cache line that may be used in the near future.

Load accesses: the time required to execute a memory load varies depending on the memory hierarchy, the accessed address and the corresponding cache behavior (hit or miss). As a result, the pipeline must be stalled when the load instruction is executed. But, to reach a higher performance, the decode stage will decode further instructions until the load has reached the memory access stage and then the pipeline will be stalled. If a memory that is shared between instructions and data at any level of the memory hierarchy is used, a conflict between instruction fetching and the load instruction may occur.

In general, both problems can be solved by the WCET analysis but depending on the memory hierarchy, it may be difficult and/or the analysis may not be very tight.

3.1.1.1. *Memory load accesses*

In case of a load access, the WCET tool must be aware of the arbitration between instruction fetching and data accesses at the point of the conflict. If separated caches that access the same memory are used, the conflict occurs only if both caches have a miss. Hence, the cache analysis should be reliable, because a conflict must be assumed at any time an unpredictable instruction fetch occurs in parallel with an unpredictable data access. Moreover, the arbitration is relevant only if the two accesses arrive at the arbiter at the same time. If the higher prioritized access arrives after the resource is granted to the lower access, the higher access has to wait until the access with the lower priority releases the required resource.

At first glance, a way to decrease the maximum access time for the high-priority access in such a situation might be to cancel the lower priority access. But this technique is not feasible for devices (dynamic RAM memories) containing an inner state. If the access is cancelled after the row of the memory is already selected, the high-priority access has to precharge the previously selected row and select the row required by itself. As a result, the lower priority access has to reselect its row again. Hence, the time required to execute both accesses is increased by the additional row selection and the required precharge. In general, both accesses are essential for the further program execution, e.g. an outstanding memory access has to be performed as well as new instructions having to be fetched. If one of these accesses is delayed, the overall program execution may be stalled. The improved execution time of one access is lapsed.

Conflicts between data and instruction fetch accesses can be dramatically reduced if an instruction scratchpad (see section 4.2) or a method cache is used. If the currently executed instructions are located inside the scratchpad or cache, no conflicts with fetches occur at the memory interface. As a method cache or a function scratchpad accesses the memory only at function boundaries, a conflict can be prohibited. This is because load/store instructions are executed in the same pipeline stage as call/return instructions. Hence, they exclude each other.

If a pipelined implementation of a processor is used, the memory announcement required for delaying the *refresh* command of a dynamic RAM can be generated easily (see section 4.3.2). This is because the memory access is already recognized by the decode stage while it is routed to the memory controller after the address is calculated in the execution stage. Hence, the occurrence of a memory access is known in advance and can be announced to the memory controller.

3.1.1.2. *Branch handling*

In case of a branch, the instruction that is unnecessarily fetched can be used reasonably if the so-called branch delay slots are part of the processor's architecture. Depending on the architecture, the length of the branch delay slot may be a single instruction or correspond to the number of cycles required to resolve a conditional branch. With respect to a tight WCET analysis, a single delay instruction is sufficient. This is because the decode stage is able to stall the fetch process directly after receiving the branch instruction, i.e. at the time the fetch of the delay instruction is started.

Being state of the art, the MIPS instruction set architecture [MIP 09] supports a single instruction inside the delay slots of branches and jumps. This instruction is executed always independent from the outcome of the branch. Aside from the always - executed delay instructions, some (older) MIPS architectures also support the so-called *likely* branches: using this type of branch, the instruction inside the delay slot is executed only if the branch is taken. This means, the delay instruction is part of the target basic block and not of the basic block following the branch. As a result, the execution time of a taken branch is drawn nearer to the execution time of a non-taken branch. While the *likely* branches are obsolete in the MIPS instruction set architecture, the SPARC architecture still supports this feature (called *anulling* [WEA 94]).

Processors that do not support a branch delay slot have to flush the pipeline after a taken branch or jump is executed. Hence, the additionally fetched instruction is also cancelled. But, if the branch has not to be taken, the additional instruction is part of the correct execution path and it does not have to be fetched again. A comparison of both techniques with respect to their performance is presented by [CME 91] showing that supporting no branch delay slot is beneficial.

Unfortunately, regarding the WCET, the instruction after the branch or jump must be always fetched, but only executed in some cases. Hence, the WCET analysis of the branch instruction must take the additional fetching into consideration. As a result, when analyzing the following basic block, the time required to fetch the first instruction is already taken into account. But, this is only true if the branch is the only dominator of the following basic block.

In contrast, the assured execution of the instruction allows the compiler to select an instruction that is executed in any case resulting in no additional overhead. Of course, the compiler must be able to determine an appropriate instruction, otherwise an artificial nop must be inserted resulting in an overhead anyway. To address this problem, several branch and jump instructions are available with and without branch delay slots in some instruction set architectures.

3.1.2. *Modeling for timing analysis*

3.1.2.1. *Execution cost of a basic block*

In a pipeline, the execution of one basic block partially overlaps the execution of the preceding basic block. Hence, what should be analyzed is not the exact execution times of basic blocks but rather their execution cost, as illustrated in Figure 3.2. The execution cost of a basic block is defined as the time interval between the terminations of the last instruction of the basic block and the last instruction of its predecessor.

The execution cost of a basic block through a simple pipeline can be computed using reservation tables, as suggested in [LIM 95]. A reservation table shows the occupancy of pipeline stages during the processing of sequences of instructions. This is illustrated in Figure 3.3 where a three-stage pipeline with two functional units (latency: four cycles), and a sequence of three basic blocks of one instruction each are considered. Building the reservation table for a basic block gives it raw execution time, and building it for two subsequent basic blocks makes it possible to derive the cost of the second one, accounting for the pipeline overlapping effect. The cost of a basic block depends on its predecessor. Then, blocks that have several predecessors in the control flow graph (CFG) may have several costs. To handle this, the costs are linked to the CFG edges instead of nodes and the integer linear programming (ILP) formulation of WCET computation is changed accordingly (total execution time computed from the execution costs and counts of edges instead of nodes).

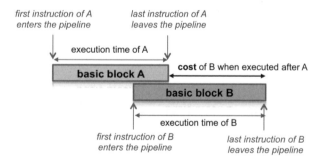

Figure 3.2. *Execution cost of a basic block*

In [ENG 99], Engblom and Ermedahl highlight that the history that impacts the execution cost of a basic block may be longer than *one* preceding basic block, i.e. the cost of a basic block can be influenced by a much earlier basic block. This phenomenon is referred to as the *long timing effect*. In [ENG 02], long timing effects are defined as follows:

A long timing effect can occur for a sequence of instructions $I_1, \ldots, I_m$ (with $m \geq 3$) only if I_1 stalls the execution of some instruction in $I_2, \ldots, I_m$, or I_1 is finally parallel to $I_2, \ldots, I_m$.

Possible long timing effects challenge the techniques used to determine the worst-case costs of basic blocks. Earlier techniques [LIM 95, LIM 98] only consider the immediate predecessors of each basic block. But this may produce unsafe execution time estimations, as illustrated in Figure 3.4 where the same pipeline and sequence of three basic blocks as in Figure 3.3 are considered. The reservation table built for the full sequence shows that the effective cost of third basic block depends not only on the second, but also on the first basic block.

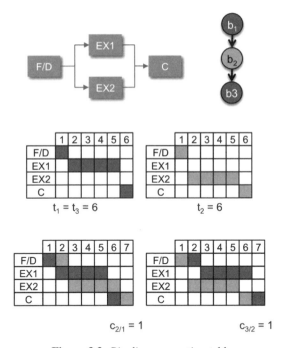

Figure 3.3. *Pipeline reservation tables*

To get safe estimates, all the predecessors, up to the first basic block of the program, should then be considered. Unfortunately, it is not possible to bound the range of a timing effect (i.e. its possible impact on the cost of a basic block), or its length (i.e. the distance between the block that generates the effect and the block that incurs it). As a result, a safe estimate of worst-case costs requires considering all the possible histories. This goes against the basic principle of static analysis, which is to avoid unrolling all the possible paths. To tackle this issue, several approaches have been proposed as discussed below.

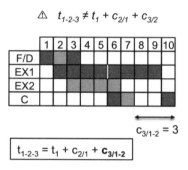

Figure 3.4. *Example of a long timing effect*

3.1.2.2. *Global analysis using abstract interpretation techniques*

The first approach [SCH 99, THE 04] uses abstract interpretation [COU 77] to compute invariants, i.e. properties that are true for any execution of the program. An example of invariant could be: "at this point in the program control flow graph, register r8 always contains a positive value". The concrete semantics of the program defines a sequence of possible consecutive program/hardware states (a trace) of an execution of the program. The collecting semantics, expressed as fixpoints, determines the set of all the possible concrete states at a given program point. From such a set at the entry of a basic block, it is possible to determine all its possible execution time (cost) values. However, in order to enhance computability, the use of an abstract semantics is preferred. It is built as a superset of the collecting semantics: at a given program point, the abstract state includes every possible concrete state. It might also include concrete states that are not feasible, this might degrade the accuracy but does not impair correctness. Usually, the concrete/abstract semantics does not represent all the aspects of the execution, but rather focuses on those that are needed to compute the desired invariant.

To analyze the behavior of the pipeline, the semantics should make it possible to detect stalls, e.g. due to control or data dependencies. Therefore, the resource demand of each kind of instruction is described. A concrete pipeline state expresses the current and future allocation of resources to active instructions. Since the number of possible states at a given program point is usually limited (at least for pipelines which are not too complex), an abstract state can be defined as the set of possible concrete states. An *update* function is used to compute the new pipeline state when an instruction enters the pipeline. A *join* function combines abstract states at path merging points. From the abstract state of the pipeline in input of a basic block, its cost can be computed. This approach is implemented in the AbsInt's aiT tool.

3.1.2.3. *Local analysis based on execution graphs*

The two other approaches perform a local analysis of pipeline states at program points, as opposed to the previous method that is based on iterative fixpoint computation. They both build an execution graph [FIE 01] for each basic block. In this graph, each node stands for the processing of one instruction in a pipeline stage or a functional unit. Directed edges express precedence constraints between nodes: they can be related to the program order (e.g. instructions are fetched in order), to the structure of the pipeline (e.g. an instruction must be fetched before being decoded), to capacity-limited instruction queues or to data dependencies. To illustrate this, we consider a simple processor including a three-stage scalar pipeline (fetch, execute and commit) with in-order execution, two functional units with a fixed latency of one cycle and a four-entry instruction window (buffer that stores all the instructions simultaneously active in the processor). This processor is illustrated in Figure 3.5. Figure 3.6 shows the execution graph of a five-instruction basic block executed on this processor. The horizontal edges express the processing flow through the pipeline, while the vertical edges express the program order or the data dependencies (e.g. edge $MEM(i0) \rightarrow ALU(i1)$). The four-instruction capacity of the instruction window is denoted by edge $CM(i0) \rightarrow IF(i4)$.

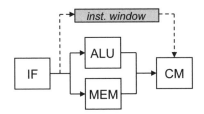

Figure 3.5. *Example of three-stage pipeline*

Analyzing the execution pattern of a basic blocks means determining the time at which each node in the execution graph can be processed. If the pipeline is empty when the block starts its execution, the processing time of each node can be computed by propagating the processing times of preceding nodes (following the graph edges) increased by the node latencies. To compute the execution cost of the basic block, its preceding instructions (also referred to as *prologue*) should also be represented. Then, the cost can be computed as the difference between the respective times of the last nodes of the basic block and of the prologue (corresponding to their last instructions leaving the pipeline). Now, the pipeline is not empty when a block starts executing and this must be taken into account. This is where the two methods differ.

i_0: r0 ← MEM[@x]
i_1: r1 ← r0 + 8
i_2: r2 ← MEM[@y]
i_3: r3 ← r10 + 12
i_4: r4 ← r2 + r3

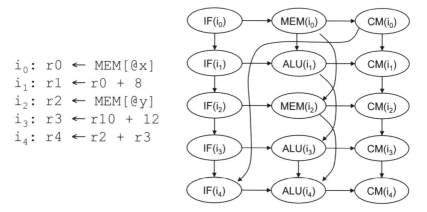

Figure 3.6. *Example of an execution graph*

In [LI 06], a worst-case initial state is considered: the latest (respectively, earliest) resource release times that are possible considering the graph precedence edges are assumed when propagating times among the nodes that stand for the basic block (respectively, prologue). Then, the worst-case cost of the block is given by the difference between the worst-case processing time of the last node of the block and the best-case processing time of the last node of the prologue. This solution is used in the Chronos tool [LI 07].

Instead of systematically considering the worst-case initial pipeline state, which may be never encountered in practice, another method consists of representing the initial state as a set of parameters that stand for the release times of hardware resources by previous basic blocks [ROC 09]. Hardware resources include not only pipeline stages, functional units, slots in instruction queues, but also register values. Their release times are expressed with respect to the start of the analyzed basic block. The processing times of the graph nodes are then computed as delays after the release times. This is shown in Figure 3.7, where the code of Figure 3.6 is prefixed by a single-instruction prologue (i_{-1}) and runs on the pipeline shown in Figure 3.5.

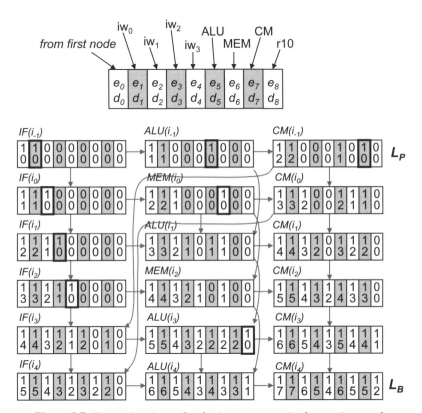

Figure 3.7. *Processing times of nodes in a parameterized execution graph*

The virtual node on top of the figure specifies the different context parameters or resource release times (iw_s stands for slot s of the instruction window). The processing time of a node is depicted by a set of pairs, each corresponding to one resource. The first item of the pair is a Boolean value that indicates whether the processing time of the node depends on the resource release time. The second item shows the minimum delay between the release of the resource and the processing of the node. For each resource (parameter), a thick-line frame indicates the first node that requires it. For example, the delays for node ALU(i_4) mean that this node can start *at the earliest*:

– six cycles after IF(i_{-1});

– four cycles after slot iw_2 of the instruction window has been released (this comes from an indirect dependency on IF(i_1));

– four cycles after the ALU has been released (this comes from path ALU(i_{-1})-CM(i_{-1})-IF(i_3)-IF(i_4)-ALU(i_4)) and three cycles after the MEM unit has been released (path MEM(i_0)-ALU(i_1)-ALU(i_3)-ALU(i_4));

– three cycles after the release of the commit stage due to the limited capacity of the instruction window;

– one cycle after r10 has been produced due to a data dependency on ALU(i_3) that itself uses register r10.

If the release times (r_i) of the set $\mathcal{R}$ of available resources were exactly known, the processing time of node n could be computed as:

$$t_n = \max_{i \in \mathcal{R}}(e_i^n.(r_i + d_i^n))$$

Now, the release times are not known in local computations. Again, the cost of a basic block is the difference between the execution times of the last nodes of the block itself (denoted by B) and its prologue (denoted by P). If they both depend on the same resources ($\forall i \in \mathcal{R}, e_i^B = e_i^P$), the cost could be computed as:

$$cost = \max_{i \in \mathcal{R}}(e_i^n.(d_i^B - d_i^P))$$

In other cases, it is shown in [ROC 09] that:

$$cost \leq \max_{i \in \mathcal{R}}(e_i^B.(d_i^B - e_i^P.d_i^P - (1 - e_i^P).d_\lambda^P))$$

where λ is the resource related to the last pipeline stage ($\forall i \in \mathcal{R}, r_i \leq r_\lambda$). As a result, an upper bound of the basic block cost can be computed without precisely knowing the pipeline state when the block starts (i.e. the resource release times). The OTAWA tool uses this approach [BAL 11].

3.1.3. *Recommendations for predictability*

A pipelined processor offers a dramatically increased performance compared to non-pipelined processors. Unfortunately, this performance boost comes along with the so-called pipeline effects that complicate the WCET analysis. Namely, these effects are conflicts at the memory interface between instruction fetching and data accesses as well as possibly needless fetches of instructions after a branch or jump.

Both effects can be addressed by some architectural adjustments. For example, a function scratchpad/cache is suitable for decoupling instruction fetching from data accesses in an analyzable way. Unnecessarily fetched instructions after branches and jumps can be converted into useful instructions by introducing branch delay slots. This technique requires that the instruction following a branch or jump be executed definitively. Hence, the compiler must select one instruction out of the basic block preceding the branch/jump and place this instruction after the branch/jump.

Applying these two techniques to a pipelined processor will reduce the overestimation of a static WCET analysis. At first glance, the use of a fetch accelerator on function granularity makes a branch delay slot dispensable. However, the instruction in the delay slot enables the compiler to move the branch/jump one instruction ahead resulting in a shorter execution time of the whole basic block.

3.2. Superscalar architectures

A further technique to increase the performance of a processor is to apply parallel execution of multiple instructions. Therefore, the front-end of the pipeline is able to fetch multiple instructions in parallel, e.g. four instructions that are also decoded in parallel and stored in a so-called issue window. The back-end comprises multiple execution units, which can be specialized units or general purpose units.

An issue stage between the front-end and the back-end assigns several instructions located in the issue window to the execution stage. Besides the capabilities of the functional units, the availability of the instructions' operands is also important for the assignment. In particular, it is not possible to issue instructions that depend on the output of currently executed or waiting instructions. Regarding the issue policy, two techniques exist that are discussed in the following sections.

3.2.1. *In-order execution*

The so-called *in-order* execution strategy issues instructions to the execution units in the same order as they are given by the instruction stream. If it is not possible to issue an instruction because of dependencies or resource conflicts, the issuing stalls. Execution units that are unused at that time remain idle for the current clock cycle. Further instructions are issued in the next pipeline cycle if the resource conflicts and the dependencies are resolved.

Speculative execution can occur in combination with branch prediction. In this case, instructions out of the predicted execution path are fetched and may be executed in parallel to the corresponding branch itself. If the branch was wrongly predicted, the instructions associated with the wrong execution path would have to be annulled or deleted from the issue window. Because of the higher fetch bandwidth of superscalar processors compared to a single-issue pipeline, the number of wrongly fetched instructions is higher. Hence, the following two major issues complicate the WCET analysis:

1) The dispensable instructions are fetched out of the instructions cache. Thus, the state of the cache strongly depends on the branch prediction.

2) Within the speculatively fetched instructions, another branch may be fetched. This additional branch is also predicted and instructions from the resulting execution path are also fetched. Hence, a further uncertainty is added to the instruction cache's state.

As a result, the state of the instruction cache cannot be analyzed in a stand-alone way anymore. The reason is the strong dependency between the cache and the branch prediction, which in turn mostly depends on the input data. Thus, very pessimistic values must be assumed for the WCET analysis.

Moreover, Wenzel *et al.* [WEN 05] have shown that timing anomalies can occur at in-order architectures if special architectural preconditions are fulfilled. In a simplified way, these preconditions are as follows:

– Multiple execution units must be able to execute the same kind of instructions, i.e. at least one instruction can be executed by more than one execution unit.

– Instruction issuing must be done in a dynamic way.

– At least one instruction shows a variable execution time, e.g. a *load* instruction has different execution times depending on the data cache state.

Figure 3.8 shows four instructions executed by two execution units (FU1 and FU2). Instruction C can be executed by FU1 or FU2. In the first case, instruction B required only one execution cycle resulting in an eight cycle overall execution time. The second case shows the instruction assignment in the case that B requires three cycles. Now, the overall execution time is shortened to seven cycles, showing that assuming the maximum execution time for each instruction separately may underestimate the WCET.

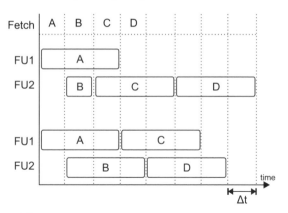

Figure 3.8. *Timing anomalies in a superscalar in-order processor showing a decreased execution time if maximum execution time of individual instructions is assumed*

If one of the mentioned preconditions is not fulfilled, timing anomalies cannot occur at in-order architectures. Hence, an in-order processor that is free of timing anomalies has to have a fixed assignment of instruction type and execution unit or it must not support dynamic instruction issuing, e.g. like a *very long instruction word* (VLIW) processor. Another possibility is to get rid of variable execution times that are not known statically.

The number of instructions with variable execution times can be reduced essentially if techniques presented in Chapter 4 are applied. Herewith, a better analysis of the memory hierarchies (instruction and data path) can be reached as well as a synchronization of the processor and the memory refreshes. Of course, the complexity of the WCET analysis increases dramatically, but timing anomalies are no longer *anomalies* because they can be predicted statically.

3.2.2. *Out-of-order execution*

In contrast to in-order superscalar processors, out-of-order architectures do not stop issuing new instructions to the execution units when a resource conflict arises. Instead, they try to issue independent instructions without resource conflicts even if these instructions are fetched after the currently conflicting instruction. As a result, the instructions of a sequential instruction stream do not pass the execution units in the same order as they entered the pipeline originally.

In the general case, out-of-order processors offer a higher performance than their in-order equivalents, but concerning their real-time capabilities, they suffer from the out-of-order feature. Timing anomalies are no longer the exception, but rather the normal case. This is because if one instruction finishes after a short execution time while the immediately following instruction cannot be scheduled, a future instruction may be issued to an execution unit. If the originally following instruction requires the same execution unit, it has to wait until the future instruction releases the concerned resource. Figure 3.9 shows a similar case. If instruction A is executed within one cycle, the complete sequence requires 10 clock cycles. Otherwise, if the execution of A is delayed, C can be executed before B resulting in a shorter overall execution time. Hence, to determine the worst-case execution path of a sequence of instructions, multiple issuing orders must be taken into account, which can result in an exploration space explosion [THE 04].

Besides distinctive timing anomalies, the so-called long timing effects can also occur. If an instruction of one basic block influences the execution of an instruction of another distant basic block, it is called a long timing effect. The second basic block may not only be a succeeding block, but also a preceding block because of the out-of-order execution. Rochange and Sainrat [ROC 05] addressed the problem of long timing effects by regulating the instruction flow through the pipeline.

The regulation method interrupts decoding new instructions at every basic block boundary if an effect of the former basic block on the new instructions is able to happen. Basic block boundaries are marked by *jump* or *branch* instructions. If necessary, artificial *jumps* have to be inserted to enable the decode unit to recognize the end of a basic block. Rochange and Sainrat propose to interrupt decoding as long as at least one resource is blocked that may be required by any possible instruction that can enter the pipeline in the next cycle. In addition, the worst-case availability times of these resources are taken into account. The authors showed through several examples that the regulation method eliminates all long timing effects within a distance of a maximum of 11 basic blocks. Longer block sequences are not evaluated because of the high computational effort required to simulate all possible combinations.

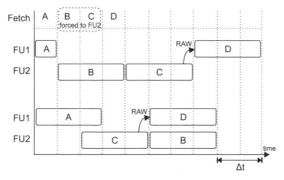

Figure 3.9. *Timing anomalies in a superscalar out-of-order processor*

Although the decoding regulation allows a higher tightness of the WCET analysis, the authors showed that using a superscalar out-of-order processor is not always a good choice. The evaluation of the performance of the regulation method compared to a simple single-issue pipeline highlights that the maximum speedup is approximately 2.3 while the minimum is less than 0.4, depending on the benchmark. Accordingly, a single-issue pipeline would deliver a higher real-time performance for some applications than an out-of-order processor.

The long timing effects inside a superscalar out-of-order pipeline can be handled by the proposed regulation method. But unfortunately, several components outside the pipeline such as caches and dynamic scratchpad RAMs also contain an inner state (that is not taken into account by the latter work). In combination with speculative execution, which is a must for out-of-order processors to reach the desired performance, these states are changed by speculatively executed instructions.

As an example, we assume a *load* instruction that is on the wrongly-predicted execution path after a branch. We also assume that the required address is already available and the load/store unit of the processor is free. Hence, the *load* is immediately executed and the address is sent to the data cache. In the simple case, the data are already in the cache and a hit occurs. Unfortunately, the cache does not know about the *speculative* state of the load and updates the replacement information in the usual way. As a result, the cache state depends strongly on the branch prediction, that in turn depends on the execution characteristics such as the code placement, the input data and, of course, the cache state, which is partly responsible for the time when branches are resolved.

This example shows that a tight analysis of a complete out-of-order system is at least very complex or even impossible. Burns *et al.* [BUR 00] modeled a moderately complex out-of-order processor (without caching effects). They underestimated the real WCET in every case by at least 0.5% and excused this problem with the following sentence: "The errors are due to the non-determinism that is left in the model and are due to arbitration occurring mainly during branching and speculation". Unfortunately, *branching* and *speculation* is the strength of an out-of-order processor and cannot be omitted.

Li *et al.* [LI 06] modeled an out-of-order processor together with branch prediction and instruction cache. They used the SimpleScalar simulator as a processor model, which simulates an abstract out-of-order processor [BUR 97]. The authors described a method to deal with timing anomalies without evaluating every possible execution path individually. Rather, they determine the interval at which an instruction can enter and leave different pipeline stages. Hence, the effort for the WCET analysis is reduced dramatically. The weak points of that work are as follows:

1) A very abstract and simple model of an out-of-order processor is used. The SimpleScalar simulator is designed for simulating different high-performance techniques, but for real-time evaluations, a high timing accuracy is required. Hence, for the WCET analysis, the authors modeled an abstract model of a processor, which is much simpler than modeling a real target processor. Inaccuracies occur in both modeling steps.

2) To ease the analysis, the authors restricted the speculation level to only a single unresolved branch. This assumption is valid for short pipelines like the SimpleScalar, but the performance of real processors with a deep pipeline (10 or more stages) would extremely suffer from this restriction.

3) The presented approach uses time intervals in which instructions enter and leave pipeline stages. These intervals are determined by evaluating the current and the preceding basic blocks. Long timing effects are not taken into account. A more extensive analysis would be required.

4) The interval methodology sounds very promising, but with regard to the long timing effects, it is not clear if it is still valid. Especially, when using a more advanced processor model, more complex resource contention will occur.

3.2.3. *Modeling for timing analysis*

The phenomenon of timing anomalies was first mentioned by Graham [GRA 69] in the context of task scheduling, then much later by Lundqvist and Stenström [LUN 99b] for dynamically scheduled processors. Often, instructions exhibit variable latencies. For example, for instruction fetches (or loads/stores), it cannot be assumed that the instruction (or data) always hits or misses in the cache levels. The behavior may instead vary along the program execution. It is tempting to consider the miss case as the worst case, since it generates the longest latency. However, this may not be valid. In [LUN 99b], timing anomalies are defined as follows:

> Considering a sequence of instructions, a timing anomaly refers to one of the two following situations: (1) an increase by a cycles of the latency of the first instruction in the sequence leads to a decrease or to an increase by more than a cycles of the execution time of the whole sequence; (2) a decrease by d cycles of the latency of the

first instruction in the sequence leads to an increase or to a decrease by more than d cycles of the execution time of the whole sequence.

Another intuitive definition is provided by Reineke [REI 06]:

A timing anomaly is a situation where the local worst-case does not entail the global worst-case.

Then, it may not be safe to consider that the worst-case latency of a memory access is that of a cache miss. More generally, every variable latency should be considered with caution. Several papers [EIS 06, KIR 09] analyze the conditions for the occurrence of timing anomalies. The objective is to identify criteria to determine whether a specific processor can be subject to such anomalies or not. But unless a very simple architecture be considered, it seems hard to prove the absence of timing anomalies.

Taking timing anomalies into account in WCET analysis requires considering every possible latency value when determining the cost of a basic block. Then, the maximum cost can be considered in the global computation. Alternatively, different cost values can be considered with appropriate constraints added to the ILP formulation of the WCET computation, as reported in [OZA 09]. In [REI 09], a different approach based on discarding non-local worst-case states in an abstract interpretation has been presented.

3.2.4. *Recommendations for predictability*

Superscalar processors are the state of the art in desktop and high-performance computing. Especially, out-of-order processors are the main representatives in these domains. With respect to the real-time capability, they suffer from their special feature: the execution of multiple instructions out of the original program order within a single clock cycle. This feature itself makes a suitable WCET analysis extremely hard. Several architectural changes such as the decoding regulation ease the analysis but at a high price in terms of performance.

In addition to the pipeline itself, the memory subsystem brings extra uncertainty into the analysis. But, for example, assuming the worst-case latency for each uncertain memory access is not allowed because of the timing anomalies that can arise if the instruction is executed faster.

In contrast to out-of-order processors, in-order processors can be designed in a more predictable way. Therefore, the preconditions shown in section 3.2.1 must be fulfilled leading to a processor without any timing anomalies. Hence, the analysis of the memory subsystem is no more critical then using an out-of-order processor. Assuming the worst-case latency for an unknown cache access can be accepted now.

Moreover, as shown by Rochange and Sainrat [ROC 05], the (real-time capable) performance of a modified (regulated decoding) out-of-order processor may be less than that of a single-issue pipeline[1] even if perfect caches are assumed. An in-order superscalar processor should also be able to reach this performance or even to outperform the real-time performance of an out-of-order processor. This is because an in-order (superscalar) pipeline with only a single execution unit (and hence, no more superscalar) is nearly identical to a simple single-issue pipeline. Additional execution units that are used only in a few but predictable cases noticeably improve the performance.

In conclusion, for the current state of technology, in-order processors are much more suitable for real-time systems than out-of-order systems. A lot of work has been done on analyzing out-of-order processors, but most of it focuses only on parts of the system. Because each subsystem influences one or more different subsystems, further work has to be done on the architectural level as well as on the basis of the WCET analysis tools to improve the real-time capabilities of out-of-order systems.

3.3. Multithreading

Multithreading was introduced to speed up the execution of multiple threads. A survey of several multithreaded architectures has been given by Ungerer *et al.* [UNG 03]. The main idea was to utilize the latency cycles resulting, e.g., from cache misses or conditional branches (in case of no branch prediction) of one thread with the execution of instructions from another thread. If this technique is applied extensively, all pipeline stages are

---

1 Depending on the application.

busy in every clock cycle. Hence, the overall number of instructions executed in 1 second is equivalent to the clock frequency (assuming a single-issue processor).

From the technological point of view, multithreaded processors offer a mechanism to switch the thread context extremely quickly. Two main types of multithreading are known: coarse-grained or block multithreading and fine-grained multithreading. Figure 3.10 shows the general execution of block and fine-grained multithreading including simultaneous multithreading (SMT). Using block multithreading, multiple instructions from the same thread are executed consecutively before a thread switch is performed. In this case, it is allowable for the thread switch to require multiple cycles (in the magnitude of one to three cycles). Instead, if fine-grained multithreading is applied, the pipeline is able to switch the context in each clock cycle. Hence, the context switch must not require any additional cycle. A further occurrence of fine-grained multithreading is the SMT whereby the multiple execution units of a superscalar processor can be used by different threads simultaneously [TUL 96a, TUL 96b, GRU 96].

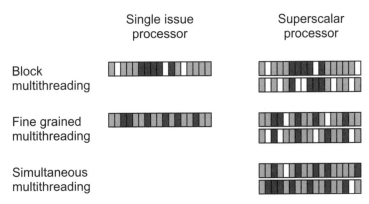

Figure 3.10. *Execution of threads with block, fine grained and simultaneous multithreading in a single-issue and a superscalar pipeline*

3.3.1. *Time-predictability issues raised by multithreading*

With respect to a real-time capable architecture, both kinds of multithreading are suitable but with one restriction for the block multithreading: because context switches are controlled and performed autonomously by the processor hardware, a static analysis of the number and the point of time of thread switches is nearly impossible. Hence, the context switch must also not require any additional time as in the case of fine-grained multithreading.

An inherent problem of multithreading is the resource sharing between different threads. Thus, interferences can occur not only between multiple instructions of a single-instruction stream but also between the instructions of different streams.

In contrast to a single thread that may be completely analyzable by a WCET tool of an arbitrary complexity, multiple interfering threads cannot be analyzed without special hardware support. This is because the interferences between threads depend on:

– the time of activation;

– the actual execution path;

– the actual timing behavior;

– the behavior of the concurrent threads.

All the mentioned topics influence the relationship of instructions of one thread to the instructions of the other threads. In particular, the resource allocation inside the pipeline, the state of the memory subsystem and the branch prediction are mainly affected. As an example, let us assume that two threads require the single multiplication unit of a processor. If both threads require the multiplication unit in the same cycle, one of them has to wait, otherwise both threads can use this unit independent of the other thread. Another example is of two consecutive memory accesses, of different threads, to the same address and, hence, to the same cache line. Depending on which thread accesses the cache first, one of the threads has a cache miss and the other thread has a cache hit. If both threads proceed with a conditional branch that also requires the same entry in the branch prediction table, the behavior will be absolutely unpredictable since the content of the branch prediction table depends on which thread resolves the branch first (and if the branch of the other thread is fetched before or after the branch is resolved).

On the basis of these examples, a real-time capable multithreaded processor architecture must provide a strict isolation of all resources for the involved threads. This means, no interferences either inside the execution stages or in the (speculation) control memories and mechanisms (like the caches and the branch prediction including related memories) are allowed. Several example architectures and approaches are briefly described in the next section.

3.3.2. *Time-predictable example architectures*

An example of a block multithreaded real-time capable processor core is the TriCore 2 from Infineon [INF]. It supports two hardware thread slots together with two execution pipelines. One at a time, instructions of only one thread enter the execution stages, i.e. it is not possible that an instruction of one thread is executed in one execution unit while the other one is used by the other thread. This is because the instructions are statically assigned to the execution units by the compiler. A special feature of the TriCore instruction set architecture is the possibility of executing two instructions simultaneously in the two execution units. In contrast to a standard superscalar processor, it is also possible under certain circumstances that the two instructions are dependent. This is obtained by a special forwarding technique from the first execution unit to the second one. The resulting timely behavior is preserved by the block multithreading technique.

Due to the in-order execution and the static assignment of the basic TriCore architecture, all preconditions mentioned in section 3.2.1 are fulfilled. Hence, no timing anomalies can occur and a static WCET analysis can be based on an instruction-by-instruction procedure. In addition, due to the strict separation of the execution of the hardware threads, no interferences between the different threads can occur inside the pipeline. The design of the memory subsystem allows us to execute one thread out of an on-chip scratchpad memory while the other thread is fetched out of the instruction cache and the external memory, respectively. This assures that no interferences in the memory system occur in the instruction path. Concerning the data path, the software developer has to take care about the real-time capability of the system.

Another example using fine-grained multithreading is the *Pret* [EDW 09] architecture described in more detail in section 6.3. This is based on a multithreaded pipeline supporting a fixed number of eight hardware thread slots. The thread scheduling performs a round-robin scheduling that switches to another thread slot in each clock cycle. Because of the fact that subsequent instructions of a thread can enter the pipeline only every eighth cycle and the short length (less than eight stages) of the pipeline, no additional features such as data forwarding, branch prediction and caches are required. Even the memory access latency is shorter than the period between two instructions of the same thread. Contention on the memory bus is avoided by forcing each thread to use its private memory bank. Hence, the row selection of a dynamic RAM of one thread is restricted to its own memory bank. No interferences between different threads can occur at this point.

The strength of the *Pret* architecture is the complete isolation of all eight threads. This isolation allows an individual WCET analysis of each thread independently. But the forced round-robin scheduling and the fixed number of threads are also a weak point, because one thread only reaches exactly one-eighth of the processor's performance; no variation is possible. In addition, the threads cannot communicate by the memory, i.e. an additional mechanism must be available to allow communication and cooperation of the threads. A special shared memory may be a solution, but in this case, a mechanism must be integrated into the processor to deal with contention on this memory.

A third example of a real-time capable multithreaded processor is the *Komodo* Java processor. It features a single-issue pipeline with multiple hard real-time capable thread scheduling algorithms. Scheduling decisions are performed on a per-cycle basis. An instruction of the winning thread is decoded in the same cycle on which the decision is made. A detailed description is given in section 6.1.

Barre *et al.* [BAR 08] propose an extension to standard multithreaded processor cores in order to allow execution of one or multiple hard real-time threads. The core supports several modes that enable the execution of zero, one, two or more (depending on the number of supported threads) hard real-time threads while the remaining threads are used for non-hard real-time threads. Buffers and queues are statically assigned to the thread slots and a low-level scheduling gives priority to the hard real-time threads. Experiments show only a negligible performance loss in case of two hard real-time threads.

3.4. Branch prediction

As stated in section 3.1, several clock cycles are required by a processor pipeline to solve a conditional branch or to determine the target address of an indirect jump. The number of cycles depends on the number of pipeline stages between the decode and the execution stage, where branches are resolved and addresses are calculated. If they are using no branch prediction, these cycles are wasted because the processor cannot perform any useful work[2].

Branch prediction has two main concerns. First, fetching the instruction that is required next can start immediately after the branch is decoded and does not have to wait until the branch is executed. Second, the spare time slots can be filled with instructions. Even if they move through the pipeline only speculatively, this is an advantage if the prediction was correct.

3.4.1. *State-of-the-art branch prediction*

In the following, the main types of branch prediction techniques are described:

Static prediction: this kind of branch prediction always supposes the same behavior. A branch is assumed to be taken or not depending on the architecture.

Direction-based prediction: using this version of branch prediction, the branch is predicted to be *taken* if it is a backward branch, otherwise as *not taken*. The main idea is to speed up the backward branch of loops.

Static compiler based prediction: an additional bit in the opcode is used by the compiler to control the predication logic of the processor. For example, if the bit is set, the processor assumes a *taken* branch.

Dynamic prediction: many techniques exist for implementing a dynamic branch prediction. Well-known techniques use a history memory in which the preceding behavior of a branch is recorded. The actual branch is predicted depending on its former behavior or that of other preceding branches. Because the size of the history memory is restricted, multiple branches must share a memory region.

---

2 This is only true for single-threaded processors. Regarding multithreaded processors, see section 3.3.

The dynamic branch prediction offers the biggest advantages in terms of average performance. Hence, it is used in most of the modern high-performance processors. Figure 3.11 shows two common types of branch predictors. A 1 bit predictor always predicts the preceding behavior of the branch as shown in Figure 3.11(a). In contrast, the 2 bit predictor requires two consecutively wrongly-predicted branches to change its behavior (Figure 3.11(b)).

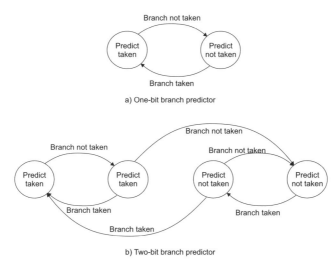

Figure 3.11. *Two types of branch predictors: the 1 bit predictor and the 2 bit predictor*

In combination with branch prediction, the so-called branch target buffers (BTBs) or branch target instruction caches (BTICs) are frequently applied. These additional buffers/caches allow us to reduce the latency of a correctly predicted taken branch to nearly zero cycles. Within these buffers, the address of the branch instruction is stored together with the target address (BTB) or the target instruction (BTIC), respectively. If the fetch stage of the processor pipeline fetches an instruction from an address already present in the BTB/BTIC, it recognizes that the corresponding instruction is a branch. After the branch prediction has predicted the branch as being taken, the fetch stage is able to fetch the next instruction from the correct target address (BTB) or it can deliver the target instruction immediately (BTIC).

The BTB as well as the BTIC lapse the branch delay slot described in section 3.1.1.2 in high-performance processor architectures.

3.4.2. *Branch prediction in real-time systems*

The high complexity of dynamic branch prediction techniques is the reason why these techniques are not suitable for real-time applications that require a tight WCET analysis. The problem is threefold:

1) Creating an exact model of a dynamic branch predictor used in modern processors is hard because the techniques are disclosed very seldom or described imprecisely.

2) If an exact model were available, dynamic branch predictors would use a global prediction table, wherein several branch instructions share the same entry. Hence, the code placement must be known and all branches that share the same entry require being analyzed by the WCET tool. An incorrect estimation of one of the branches leads to an incorrect WCET estimation of other branches.

3) If the applied branch predictor is a so-called two-level predictor, it uses the branch history (besides the branch address) as input to the prediction table. Hence, the behavior of the preceding branches must also be known. In case of a global branch history, all branches share a single history register, i.e. the prediction of one branch is based on the directly preceding branch instructions. In contrast, using a local or private history, the prediction focuses on the previous behavior of only the actual branch instruction. Again, several instructions may share the same history register in the prediction table.

If the decision of the branch prediction cannot be determined by the WCET analysis, a misprediction has to be assumed. In addition to the prediction, the WCET tool must also determine the actual behavior of the branch itself in order to update the prediction table of the internal model. Hence, the WCET tool must perform an exact static analysis of the execution of each branch. If this is not possible, each branch must be regarded as being mispredicted, which results in a high overestimation.

Static branch prediction techniques are much more suitable for real-time systems, independent of the type of prediction. Apart from the more precise WCET estimation, it is also possible to reduce the WCET if a compiler-based prediction is used. Bodin *et al.* [BOD 05] present a technique that analyzes and optimizes a real-time application using compiler-based static branch prediction. This technique determines the worst-case execution path and directs the static prediction to the longer execution path. Hence, a possible misprediction penalty has no (or only a minor) effect on the worst-case path. Since changing the prediction direction of one branch may have an effect on the overall WCET, the proposed algorithm has to be applied iteratively.

An approach to deal with dynamic branch prediction is proposed by Burguière *et al.* [BUR 05a]. They determine an upper bound of mispredictions for an inner nested loop with an arbitrary (but bounded) number of iterations. The analyzed branch predictor is a 2 bit predictor without history. Even this comparably simple predictor requires a complex model that does not take into account other branches sharing the same prediction table entry. Of course, if the model is applied to inner loops without internal branches and subroutine calls, this assumption is completely valid as no other branch can harm the prediction table.

3.4.3. *Approaches to branch prediction modeling*

The static analysis of a dynamic branch predictor can be local or global. A *local* analysis considers each conditional branch in isolation. It determines its behavior relatively to the algorithmic structure it implements. For example, a conditional branch located in a loop header is not taken while the loop iterates and taken at the loop exit. Models for various algorithmic patterns considering 1 bit or 2 bit branch predictors are provided in [COL 00], [BAT 05] and [BUR 05b]. By definition, local analyses do not fit history-based prediction schemes that exploit correlations among successive branches.

A *global* analysis determines the behavior of a given branch taking into account the other branches. In [LI 05], a model for 1 bit branch predictors with a branch history table (BHT) indexed by a global history register is proposed. This approach has been extended and generalized to 2 bit predictors with various BHT indexing schemes in [MAI 11]. The global analysis of branch predictors is not performed separately, as the cache analysis is (described in Chapter 4). Instead, it is integrated as part of the WCET computation (implicit path enumeration technique (IPET)): the behavior of branches is expressed by a (large) set of additional constraints in the ILP formulation. More precisely, these constraints provide answers to the following questions, for each conditional branch in the program:

– Which entry of the BHT is used to predict the branch? Generally, the index results from a function of the branch address (PC) and of the global history (for a bimodal predictor, the function equals the branch address; for a Gshare scheme, the function is an exclusive-or of the history and significant bits of the address; for a GAg scheme, only the history is considered). Some constraints define the possible values of the index.

– Which other branches may update the same BHT entry (due to aliasing)? Possible updates on the prediction counter done by other branches must be accounted for. Some constraints express possible conflicts in the BHT.

– What can the value of the prediction counter be? Some other constraints translate the way the prediction counter is updated after a branch.

Finally, a fourth set of constraints links those of the first three sets. Further details on how these constraints can be built are given in [MAI 11]. In [BUR 07], the additional complexity of the integer linear program used to determine the WCET is evaluated in terms of the number of additional constraints (C), number of additional variables (V) and arity (A) of the system, i.e. the maximum number of variables in the same constraints. These factors intuitively act on the complexity of the problem, which was checked by observing that they are directly correlated to the resolution time. Table 3.1 shows the mean values found on a set of benchmarks from the Mälardalen suite [GUS 10], considering three indexing schemes: by the branch address (bimodal), by an exclusive-or of some bits of the address and the global branch history (Gshare) and by the global history only (GAg). It is clearly apparent that the use of a predictor with a global history register, which favors interactions among branches, dramatically increases the complexity of WCET analysis.

Bimodal			Gshare			GAg		
C	V	A	C	V	A	C	V	A
×3.4	×19.9	×3.1	×10.5	×14.6	×9.3	×27.3	×45.1	×46.0

Table 3.1. *Additional complexity of the ILP formulation with branch prediction modeling*

All the studies mentioned above, except for [COL 00], focus on the analysis of predicting branch directions (taken or not taken). Now, whenever a branch is predicted taken, the target address must be retrieved in the BTB. This should also be considered in the WCET analysis. In [COL 00], the BTB behavior is analyzed as a least recently used (LRU) cache indexed by branch addresses. A more general framework is introduced in [GRU 11a] and applied to the MPC56x BTIC (branch target instruction cache), a first in, first out (FIFO) eight-way four-entry buffer used to store target instructions.

4

Memory Hierarchy

In the space of performance increasing techniques, the memory hierarchy plays a major role. A processor can only be as fast as it retrieves the data, including the instructions. The data and instruction access is optimized by a so-called memory hierarchy as shown in Figure 4.1. Starting from the processor, the size of the available memory blocks increase up to the main memory. In parallel, the access times also increase, i.e. the smallest memory is nearest to the processor and it is the fastest one.

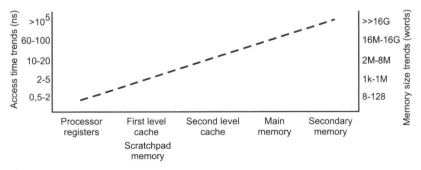

Figure 4.1. *Size and access time trends of different memories in the memory hierarchy*

The full memory hierarchy shown in Figure 4.1 spans from the register setup to a secondary storage such as a hard disc. The latter can be omitted in hard real-time systems because the total required amount of memory is known in advance and, hence, the main memory should be of sufficient size.

While the timing of the main memory, where static RAM (SRAM) as well as dynamic RAM can be used, is very complex (see section 4.3), the timing of the memory on the opposite end of the memory hierarchy, the register set, is very simple. Moreover, the timing of accesses to the register file is known to the software developer because it is part of the processor/pipeline structure as described in section 3.1.

The hierarchy levels in between the two extremes can be implemented in different ways and have a high impact on the predictability of the system. Two different types of hierarchical memory form the main possibilities: cache memories and scratchpad RAMs. Both techniques represent completely different approaches and offer advantages as well as disadvantages to hard real-time systems. They are discussed in the following sections.

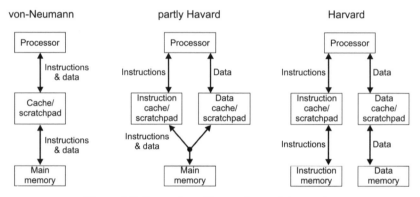

Figure 4.2. *Separation of instruction and data path*

Besides the hierarchical chaining of multiple memories, the memory access path of the processor is often at least partly divided into two parts (see Figure 4.2): the instruction and the data path. This so-called *Harvard* architecture (see Brinkschulte and Ungerer [BRI 02]) improves the performance as well as the predictability of the timing behavior. In contrast to a *von Neumann* architecture, the separation of the two paths prevents one path from interfering with the other path. With regard to the predictability of a hard real-time system, the complete separation of the two paths is optimal but not always feasible.

4.1. Caches

4.1.1. *Organization of cache memories*

Caches are dynamic memories comprising small pieces (lines) of the address range of the processor. These lines contain copies of the values stored in the main memory and the address window covered by line changes during runtime. The cache itself is not part of the address range and, hence, it is known to the software developer in principle.

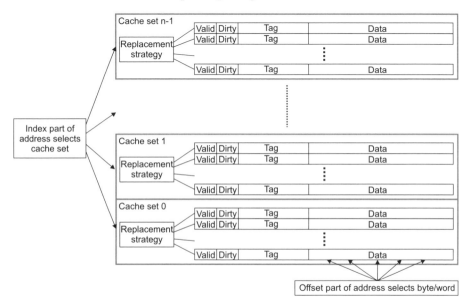

Figure 4.3. *Principal schematic of a cache*

A cache is arranged in multiple sets and each set contains at least one line as shown in Figure 4.3. The capacity of a line depends on the actual implementation, typical sizes range from 32 to 256 bytes. All lines within a set can be mapped to the identical blocks of the address range and the sets are mapped and interleaved into the address map. Figure 4.4 describes the mapping of the address range to the sets. Therefore, the address vector is divided into the following three parts:

– *Offset*: the offset indicates the byte or word that is addressed within a line. The offset is required only to select the byte/word that has to be transferred from the cache to the processor in case of a read, or that has to be changed inside the line during a write access. It has no meaning for the mapping of the line to the address range but, at several implementations, it indicates that the word has to be transferred first from the memory to the cache in case of a miss. This technique ensures that the currently required word is read first from the memory to shorten the read latency [HEN 07].

– *Index*: the index part of the address represents the set that is accessed. It is responsible for the interleaved mapping of addresses to the sets. If a continuous memory block of at least $\sharp sets * \sharp(bytes\_per\_line)$ bytes is accessed, each set is affected. In the case of multiple lines per set, not necessarily all lines are covered but the replacement strategy inside each set is concerned.

– *Tag*: the tag is the part of the address that is stored together with the data inside a cache line. At every access, the tags of all lines within a set are compared to the actual address. If one of the lines' tags match, it is called a cache hit. Otherwise, a cache miss occurs.

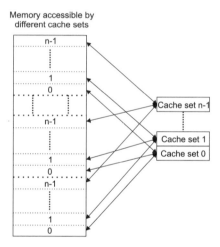

Figure 4.4. *Address mapping of a cache*

A cache with only a single line per set is called a *direct mapped cache*. Using this kind of cache, each location in the main memory is mapped exactly to one cache line. In contrast, a memory location can be mapped to any of the lines inside a set if a cache with multiple lines is used, a so-called *n-set associative cache* with n lines per set. In this case, an eviction strategy is required to select the line that is replaced by new data at the time of a cache miss. Several strategies are known that are described in the following:

– *First in, first out (FIFO), Round robin (RR)*: the FIFO/RR strategy uses one counter for each set. The counter represents the cache line that is recently filled after a cache miss. The next miss increments the counter and fills up the next line. If the counter reaches the last line, it is set to the first line again. Cache hits do not modify the counter.

– *Pseudo round robin (P-RR)*: the P-RR strategy works in a similar way to FIFO/RR. In contrast to this, P-RR uses a single counter for all cache sets while FIFO/RR uses one counter per set. As a result, cache misses in one set affect the contents and, hence, also the hit rate of all other sets.

– *Most recently used (MRU)*: the MRU strategy preserves the MRU cache line from being evicted. Therefore, a bit mask is used to mark all accessed cache lines. Each bit of the mask represents one line. If a line is accessed, the corresponding bit is set to 1. At the time the mask contains only a single 0, the mask is inverted if the line corresponding to the 0 is accessed. A cache miss selects one of the lines with a 0 to be evicted. Hence, a set of n lines contains between 0 and $n - 1$ candidates to be evicted, depending on the time of the mask's inversion and the cache miss.

– *Least recently used (LRU)*: The LRU strategy keeps a strict list of the order of used lines. If a line is used, it is moved to the beginning of that list. If a line has to be replaced, the date in the line represented by the tail of the list is evicted. Several techniques are known to implement the LRU strategy in hardware but they are very costly compared to other strategies [SUD 04].

– *Pseudo-LRU (P-LRU)*: a less complex strategy in terms of hardware cost is the pseudo-LRU strategy. This strategy guarantees that one of the lines not recently used is selected for eviction but it is not guaranteed that the LRU line is chosen. The implementation looks like a binary tree for each cache set. The leafs represent the lines. Each node contains a single bit selector that indicates the direction (left/right) of the unused cache line. If a cache hit occurs, all bits on the way from the root to the corresponding cache line are set to the direction that doesn't point to the associated line. In case of a miss, the direction bits in the nodes point to a cache line that was not recently used. Figure 4.5 shows an example with a set containing four cache lines.

To reliably predict the timing behavior of a cache access, multiple facts must be known (see Heckmann *et al.* [HEC 03]). First, it must be determined if a cache miss or hit occurs. Therefore, the architecture together with the replacement strategy and the access history must be known. In addition, the access latency in case of a hit and a miss must also be available. The latter mainly depends on the memory access timing as described in section 4.3.

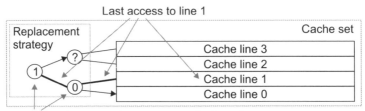

Figure 4.5. *Pseudo-LRU strategy*

The following sections present several approaches to improve WCET estimation if caches are used. The proposed techniques are based on an adapted hardware design that eases the *cache analysis*.

4.1.2. *Static analysis of the behavior of caches*

Accesses to the cache are triggered by instruction fetching and by executing memory instructions (loads and stores). For each access, the analysis must answer the following two questions:

– *What is the memory address of the access?* Provided the position of the text section in memory is known at analysis time, instruction fetches are trivially done at instruction addresses. The question is much more complex for data: the address may be dynamically computed, and then may not be available in the instruction code for the analysis. In addition, accesses to data located in loop bodies may access a different address at each iteration, e.g. when scanning an array. This makes the analysis of data caches more complex, as discussed in section 4.1.2.2.

– *Does the instruction/data reside in the cache?* Common techniques for the analysis of cache memories aim at labeling the instructions that trigger an access to the cache (instruction fetch or data load/store) with categories, as those introduced in [MUE 95]: *AlwaysHit* (for any execution of the program, the instruction or data is in the cache), *AlwaysMiss* (the instruction or data misses and must be retrieved from the higher levels of the memory hierarchy) and *NotClassified* or *Conflict* (the analysis is not able to determine a constant behavior for the access).

These categories are used to enrich the integer linear programming (ILP) formulation of WCET computation. If time composability is ensured, i.e. if the processor is free from timing anomalies (see section 3.2.3), a simple solution is to increase the WCET expression with a miss penalty for each possible miss (access classified as *AlwaysMiss* or *NotClassified*). The number of misses is trivially determined from the execution counts of the instructions that trigger an access to the cache. If the processor is instead subject to timing anomalies, the computation of the costs of basic blocks must consider any possible combination of hits and misses for the accesses generated by the block. Note that the number of possible combinations rapidly increases with the number of accesses.

To improve the precision of the analysis, a fourth category can be considered: *Persistent* (sometimes called *FirstMiss*). It concerns cache lines that are accessed in the body of a loop and remain in the cache from one iteration to the next (but may miss at the first iteration) [MUE 95], [FER 99a], [BAL 08], [CUL 13]. Section 4.1.2.1 describes how these categories can be determined using abstract interpretation techniques [COU 77].

4.1.2.1. *Analysis of instruction caches by abstract interpretation*

Processors usually issue instruction fetches to the memory hierarchy each time the control flow reaches a new cache line. For this reason, instruction cache analysis does not label individual instructions but instead *line-blocks* or shortly *l*-blocks [LI 95b]. An *l*-block results from the projection of the control flow graph (CFG) on the cache line map: it contains instructions that belong to the same basic block and to the same cache line.

Popular techniques for assigning categories to *l*-blocks are based on abstract interpretation [COU 77], as first proposed in [ALT 96a]. Fixpoint analysis is performed to determine the possible states of the instruction cache before and after each *l*-block. Usually, the number of states is very large. For this reason, an abstract domain and abstract semantics are used to keep the analysis tractable. An abstract cache state (ACS) links a set S of *l*-blocks to each cache line. For an A-way set associative cache, each *l*-block is assigned an age a with $a \in [0..A[\cup l_\top$, where virtual age $l_\top$ is the oldest possible age and is given to *l*-blocks that have been loaded and then replaced in the cache.

Three analyses are performed: *may*, *must* and *persistence*. *Update* functions determine the impact of fetching an *l*-block to the input ACS. *Join* functions merge several input ACS at junctions in the CFG.

For the may analysis, set S contains the *l*-blocks that *can* reside in the cache, and the age of an *l*-block is its youngest possible age. The update function adds the *l*-block to S (if not already present) and computes the new ages of all *l*-blocks in S. For an LRU cache, the referenced *l*-block is given age 0 and all the other *l*-blocks are aged, keeping their smaller possible age. The join function makes the union of the input ACS and keeps the lowest possible age for each *l*-block. Figure 4.6 illustrates the effects of the update and join functions for the may analysis, considering a single set in an LRU four-way associative instruction cache.

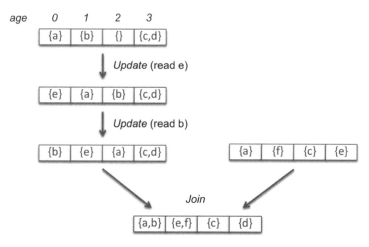

Figure 4.6. *Example of may analysis for an LRU four-way associative instruction cache*

Similarly, the must analysis considers the *l*-blocks that are *guaranteed* to be in the cache, and their age is their oldest possible age. The join function computes the intersection of the input ACS and keeps the highest possible age for each *l*-block. Figure 4.7 illustrates the effects of the update and join functions for the must analysis, still for an LRU four-way associative instruction cache.

In the persistence analysis, set S contains the *l*-blocks that may be in the cache with their oldest possible age. Each *l*-block that has an age lower than

$l_\top$ is guaranteed to remain in the cache once loaded. The update function is similar to that of the must analysis. The join function computes the union of input states and keeps the maximal age of each l-block.

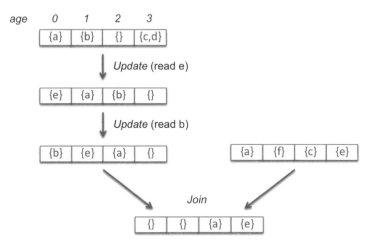

Figure 4.7. *Example of must analysis for an LRU four-way associative instruction cache*

Once built, the ACSs are used to determine the categories presented above. An l-block is labeled AlwaysHit (respectively AlwaysMiss or persistent) if it resides in the must (respectively may, persistent) ACS and if its age is not $l_\top$. In all other cases, the l-block is called NotClassified.

Figure 4.8 shows the results of cache analysis for a simple program. The CFG includes three basic blocks, each assumed to reference a single cache line. The cache is a two-way associative cache with a single set. The input and output ACS for each basic block after the must, may and persistence analyses are displayed. The cache line referenced by block a is not in the input may ACS: it is then classified as *AlwaysMiss*. The cache line fetched by block b is not in the input must ACS, but resides in the may ACS as well as in the persistence ACS. It is then classified as *persistent* or *FirstMiss*. A single miss for this cache line will be accounted for at each execution of the loop. The same happens for the cache line related to block c.

The analysis described above assumes an LRU replacement policy. Solutions have been proposed for other policies, such as FIFO [GRU 10a] and PLRU [GRU 10b]. The predictability of replacement strategies is compared in [REI 07], considering two metrics: *evict* tells how many references to a cache set are needed to evict any memory block from the may set (then any access to this block is guaranteed to miss); *fill* tells the number of different accesses after which the contents of a cache set is precisely known. They both depend on the cache associativity. They characterize the speed at which an ACS retrieves enough information to accurately classify the hit/miss behavior of an access after it has been degraded due to static analysis approximations (e.g. unions/intersections of ACS at merging points). Table 4.1 presents the predictability metrics for the LRU, FIFO and PLRU policies. It suggests that LRU is the most predictable.

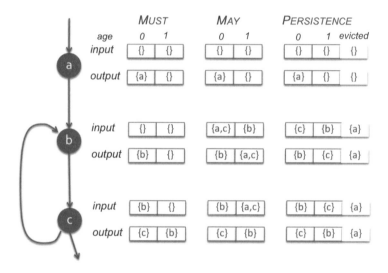

Figure 4.8. *Example of instruction cache analysis by abstract interpretation. An LRU two-way associative cache is considered*

Berg [BER 06] describes that the PLRU policy can generate *domino effects*: according to the initial state of the cache, the number of cache misses in a loop body takes different values without converging. This phenomenon is further analyzed in [REI 13] where the sensitivity of cache replacement policies to the initial state of the cache is studied. They show that the initial cache state has a strong impact on the number of hits and misses when considering the FIFO, PLRU and MRU policies. In addition, considering an empty cache as the worst initial state is not safe for these policies. This argues for favoring the LRU scheme.

Policy	$Evict(k)$	$Fill(k)$
LRU	k	k
FIFO	$2k - 1$	$3k - 1$
PLRU	$\frac{k}{2}\log_2 k + 1$	$\frac{k}{2}\log_2 k + k - 1$

Table 4.1. *Predictability metrics for three cache replacement policies [REI 07]. k is the cache associativity*

4.1.2.2. *Analysis of data caches*

The specificity of data caches is that the accessed addresses may be dynamically computed at runtime. This is the case for the following:

– Stack data, i.e. function parameters and local variables: these addresses can be determined by static analysis, as in [REG 05].

– Pointers to data: for statically allocated data, the value of pointers may be determined by a static analysis of value ranges, which can be done by abstract interpretation. Things are more complex for pointers to heap data, since their address is decided by the operating system during the execution [DUD 11]. For this reason, dynamic memory allocation should be avoided in critical software.

– Array elements accessed within a loop: each iteration of the loop may access a different element. Then, several addresses are possible for a single load/store instruction. However, their values can often be determined by value analysis [FER 98, SEN 07, HUY 11].

An unpredictable address leads to assuming a cache miss since it cannot be determined whether the data are in the cache or not. In addition, it degrades the ACS because it cannot be predicted whether it replaces another cache line, and if so, which one. It is then considered that it impacts every cache set. The knowledge of a value range for a dynamic address helps in limiting the damage to the sets to which it may map, and thus in limiting overestimation on the overall cache miss penalties.

4.1.2.3. *Impact of task pre-emption on cache analysis*

Pre-emptive task scheduling may impair the cache analyses described above: when a pre-empted task resumes its execution, it may not find the cache in the same state as it was when the task was pre-empted. This is due to the pre-empting tasks loading their own instructions/data in the cache, thus possibly replacing instructions/data belonging to the pre-empted task. For the pre-empted task, this results in additional cache misses that are not predicted by traditional cache analysis. This issue has been tackled in several papers that aim at computing the so-called *cache-related pre-emption delays* (CRPDs).

The analysis of CRPDs is based on computing sets of *evicting cache blocks* (ECB) and *useful cache blocks* (UCB) [LEE 98]. The ECBs are the cache lines that can be loaded by the task during its execution. The UCBs are the cache lines that are reused by the task after having been loaded and before being evicted by the task itself. When a UCB is replaced by another (pre-empting) task, it may have to be reloaded by the pre-empted task, and this should be accounted for as an additional delay due to pre-emption.

The computation of CRPDs is performed as part of the task response time analysis, in order to estimate the cost of pre-emptions. It considers a combination of the ECB and UCB of pre-empting and pre-empted tasks. Several approaches have been proposed for fixed-priority scheduling [BUS 96, LEE 98, TAN 07, ALT 12] and pre-emptive earliest deadline first (EDF) scheduling [LUN 13]. Optimized mapping of tasks in memory may improve their schedulability by reducing CRPDs [LUN 12].

4.1.2.4. *Analysis of multilevel cache hierarchies*

A solution to the static analysis of a hierarchy of instruction caches has been proposed in [HAR 08]. It supports *mainly inclusive* hierarchies, where the various levels of caches behave independently, i.e. where no specific action is taken to guarantee the inclusion *or* the exclusion of the contents of one cache in upper levels. The analysis process is summarized in Figure 4.9. The levels of the hierarchy are analyzed starting from the lowest level. Each access to one of the caches is assigned two categories: the first category is that used for single-level caches and denotes the hit/miss behavior of the cache for this access and the second category indicates whether an access to the upper level cache is needed (three labels are considered: *always*, *never* and *uncertain*). The two categories are combined to determine which instruction fetches reach a given level of the hierarchy.

In [LES 09], this approach is extended to data caches. A new abstraction called *live caches* is introduced in [SON 10]. It models relationships between cache levels, making it possible to consider any cache hierarchy, including inclusive and exclusive ones. It also improves the precision of the analysis.

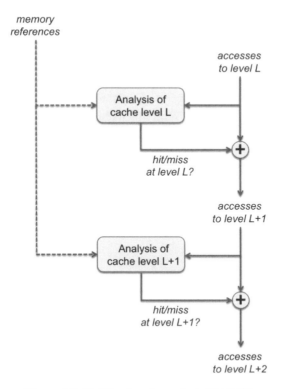

Figure 4.9. *Multilevel cache analysis [HAR 08]*

4.1.3. *Recommendations for timing predictability*

4.1.3.1. *Data cache*

One problem of data cache timing prediction is the address analysis. To perform an accurate cache analysis, the addresses of the analyzed memory accesses must be known. Unfortunately, the addresses of memory accesses may be difficult to predict. Even if slight inaccuracies occur, the concerned address is mapped to a different cache set than predicted, which leads to a wrong cache analysis.

This section presents the standard cache locking combined with a compiler technique to lock/unlock the cache at selected code structures. Moreover, two hardware techniques are proposed to ease the address and cache analysis during WCET estimation.

4.1.3.1.1. Cache locking

A technique to improve the predictability of data memory access times is cache locking. Thereby, the data cache can be locked entirely by the application or the associativity can be reduced. The cache lines no more used as associative lines are locked, i.e. their content is fixed and cannot be evicted as long as the locking is active. With this technique, it is possible to adjust the size of the data cache in cooperation with the size of the fixed content.

Unfortunately, locking the cache entirely during the complete execution time of a task leads to a high-cache miss-rate, if not all the required data fits into the cache (which will normally be the case). As a result, the task gains predictability but, on the other hand, it will nearly be as slow as not using a cache at all.

Vera *et al.* [VER 03] presented a compiler-based cache analysis that improves predictability of real-time applications with a minimal performance loss. They introduced a *lock/unlock* statement that will be integrated into the source code. The data cache is locked by the processor at the *lock* instruction and succeeding load instructions pass the cache. Hence, the state of the cache is not changed until the *unlock* instruction is executed. This technique prevents unpredictable (or at least hard to predict) memory accesses that would pollute the cache and its history/state, respectively. For example, if we assume a loop with a bounded but statically unknown concrete number of iterations that subsequently reads memory cells. As a result, the state of the cache after the loop is unknown. Putting the loop within the *lock/unlock* environment prevents the cache from being accessed and, hence, its state remains unchanged.

This technique provides the advantage of a predictable cache state assuming that it was predictable before the loop execution, leading to a more accurate WCET analysis. In addition, depending on the instructions inside the loop, it may also offer a performance improvement. If the loop accesses each cache line only once, the cache does not bring any improvement because it produces only cache misses and, moreover, it is cache pollution at least by a certain percentage. Without cache accesses during the loop, the locality characteristics before and after the loop may bring some improvements because the state of the cache is unchanged.

4.1.3.1.2. Domain caches

Further improvements in terms of predictability and an acceptable performance gain might be possible by introducing multiple data caches. These caches could be dedicated to different domains, e.g. one cache for accesses inside loops and one cache for other accesses. In this configuration, the *lock/unlock* mechanism can be modified to switch between these domains. The loop cache can be comparatively small because loops mainly iterate over a huge amount of memory that, in any case, does not fit into the cache. In addition, each line loaded into the cache is used only a few times compared to the total amount of memory accesses inside the loop.

From the point of view of static WCET analysis, the state of the loop domain cache might be regarded as unknown at the entry of a loop. Inside the loop, the analysis focuses only on the loop cache and after the loop, the general cache guarantees to have the same state as before the loop. If multiple subsequential loops are known to work on the same data, it is also possible to transfer the state of the previous loop to the next loop. In the case of nested loops, where to set the domain boundaries is open. If the inner loop might be executed millions of times while the outer loop iterates only a dozen times and offers a predictable cache state, only the inner loop should be executed using the loop cache. Otherwise, the outer loop should also be executed as a part of the loop domain.

A problem arising from the different domain caches is the cache consistency, because the same memory cell can be accessed outside as well as inside a loop. In this case, the access inside the loop must not change the state of the cache line in the other cache regarding the replacement strategy. But it is required that the data inside the corresponding cache line are updated in the case of a write operation.

Figure 4.10 shows a block diagram of a possible implementation of two domain caches. Write accesses are directed to both caches. The currently active cache handles writes like a standard cache depending on the write strategy. In contrast, the inactive cache checks the address against its content and, if necessary, updates the corresponding cache line. The state required for the replacement strategy is not modified at all.

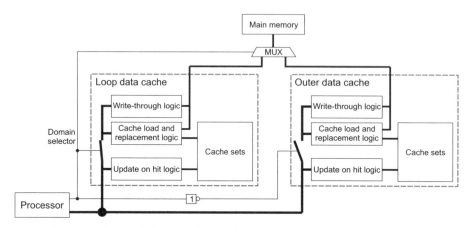

Figure 4.10. *Block diagram of a possible implementation of domain caches*

In addition, the write strategy of the caches is very important at the time of a domain switch. If a write-back strategy is performed, all cache lines marked as *modified* in the old cache must be written back to the memory before the new cache is activated. Otherwise, the new cache will read incorrect values from the memory. The write-back action should be triggered by the switching instruction. The time required for the write back should be known to the analysis tool because the number of modified cache lines can be analyzed more precisely compared to a single big data cache.

A solution, getting rid of the extra write back, is to use snooping caches. In this case, the currently inactive cache acts as a kind of second-level read cache without any influence on the timing. If a cache line is not present in the active cache, it is loaded from the memory. At the same time, the inactive cache compares its content against the requested address and, if it is available, delivers the cache line to the active cache while the data from the memory are discarded. Again, the inactive cache must not change its state.

4.1.3.1.3. Dedicated caches

Dedicated caches may be a more flexible variation of domain caches. In contrast to domain caches, where regions of the program are assigned to one or more special caches, dedicated caches allow a relationship between individual memory access instructions and caches. For example, accesses to statically assigned memory regions may use one cache while accesses to dynamically allocated arrays use other caches. Three such caches may be used to enhance predictability: one for the accesses to statically-known addresses, one for the accesses to addresses that cannot be predicted, and one for accesses to addresses that can be predicted with low accuracy.

Of course, the same cache consistency problem occurs as when using the domain cache. In addition, the write-back technique cannot be applied because of the absence of special switching instructions. Instead, a write-through policy or the snooping cache technique must be used.

To establish a relationship between memory access instruction and the appropriate cache, an annotation of the instructions is required, which should be supported by the WCET analysis tool. This annotation may be combined with the memory access announcement discussed in section 4.3.2. As a result, the timing behavior of a memory hierarchy containing the proposed dedicated data cache and a dynamic RAM can be predicted much more accurately than current standard implementations without memory announcement.

4.1.3.2. *Instruction cache*

The address analysis of instruction caches for a single task is much easier than that of data caches. This is because of the sequential instruction stream of the task that is interrupted only by known jumps and branches. Indirect jumps must be annotated by the user and/or compiler to be handled reliably by the WCET analysis. Nevertheless, multiple control flows are possible during the execution of a task that again being uncertainty, but much less than the same uncertain control flow will bring to the data cache.

4.1.3.2.1. Cache locking

Cache locking is also a suitable way for instruction caches to reach a more predictable application timing behavior. However, filling the cache with the desired values is much more complicated than using a data cache. This is because filling the data cache can be done by load instructions to the concerned memory addresses. In contrast, instructions can be moved into the instruction cache only by fetching them for execution. But executing these instructions is not desired at that point of time. As a result, a processor that supports cache locking must additionally provide a technique to fill-up the instruction cache. An alternative fill-up procedure is provided by the Freescale e300 processor core. It uses speculative execution to load the instruction cache. Thereby, a speculative branch to the desired instruction is executed, which is hence fetched into the cache. Because the speculative branch is never taken, the instruction is not executed [FRE 06]. This technique can be applied only with static speculation, a dynamic speculation technique would *learn* that the branch was never taken in the past and the branch target would not be fetched into the cache (see section 3.4).

Several approaches have been proposed to compute an optimized cache content offline. In [PUA 02a, PUA 06a], the instructions that belong to the worst-case execution path (formerly determined) are favored. In [CAM 05], a generic algorithm is used to enhance the process of selecting the instructions to be loaded in the cache. The number of WCET analyses required to recompute the worst-case execution path while determining the instruction cache contents can be reduced using execution flow graphs or trees, as in [FAL 07, LIU 09], or ILP models, as in [PLA 12].

4.1.3.2.2. Instruction clustering

Another possibility to gain a predictable cache timing behavior is to cluster the instructions semantically. For example, instructions can be grouped by their basic blocks or by the function they form. The advantage of this instruction grouping is that the static WCET analysis tool can assume cache hits for all instructions inside the group except for the first instruction. The first instruction's timing behavior has to be analyzed by control flow and cache analysis or, in the worst case, a cache miss must be assumed. The cost for a miss depends on the size of the instruction group resulting in high cost for big groups. If the group is almost completely executed, the certainty of the hits inside the group outbalances the higher miss cost. Otherwise, if the group is left shortly after its execution starts, the high miss cost cannot be argued.

In addition, the size of the groups has an impact on the WCET analysis. The entries of bigger groups, e.g., on the basis of functions are easier to analyze than small groups like basic blocks.

An example of a cache for clustered instructions is the method cache implemented in Schoeberl's Java Optimized Processor (JOP) [SCH 04b]. He developed a method cache for a Java processor. The method cache can hold multiple complete Java methods that are loaded by method invocations and returns, if required. As Schoeberl reported, the performance of a method cache is similar or at least comparable of that of a direct-mapped instruction cache of the same size.

A clear advantage of cluster-based caches is the fact that instruction transfer from the main memory to the cache takes place only at the entry points of the instruction groups, e.g. at a method or function call. This means, in contrast to a standard cache, that conflicts at the main memory cannot occur during the execution of such a group. Hence, the static WCET analysis is not required to take these conflicts into account (see section 3.1).

4.2. Scratchpad memories

4.2.1. *Scratchpad RAM*

A scratchpad RAM is a technique most often found in embedded systems. This type of memory is a special SRAM near the processor. In general, it can be accessed only by the local processor core with very fast access cycles, i.e. in the range of one or two processor cycles. In contrast to a cache memory, which has the same access properties in terms of locality and speed, the scratchpad RAM is a part of the address map. Accordingly, accesses to the scratchpad must be done explicitly by load/store/fetch accesses to an appropriate address.

Some processors contain only a single scratchpad RAM that can be used for both data and instructions alike. But because the scratchpad RAM is not cached, fetch accesses to instructions inside the scratchpad are very frequent and may conflict with possible data accesses. Hence, a *Harvard* architecture with separated instruction and data scratchpads is self-evident in terms of performance and predictability.

4.2.2. *Data scratchpad*

The challenge of data scratchpads is to determine which data to put into it. Because of its restricted size, only selected data should be located inside the scratchpad. In addition, only data locally generated and used by the processor, i.e. no input/output data, can be placed inside the scratchpad.

Because of the explicit accesses by load/store instructions, the content of the scratchpad must be determined by the developer or the compiler, i.e. it is statically defined. In conjunction with a known access time (in case of a Harvard architecture), a tight WCET analysis of the application parts accessing the scratchpad is possible. With respect to performance improvement, especially frequently used data should be located in the scratchpad. As an example, the stack may be an optimal candidate because it is accessed at least every time a function is called and at the `return` instruction. In addition, local variables that are located on the stack and are also accessed very often should be placed in the scratchpad [DEV 07]. In [SUH 05], an allocation algorithm based on integer linear programming techniques is proposed.

Another approach to determine the content of a data scratchpad is presented by Cho *et al.* [CHO 07]. They propose to use a memory management unit (MMU) to dynamically map different address ranges to the scratchpad. Although they characterize their technique as dynamic, they statically determine which address range should be mapped to the scratchpad at which time. Therefore, they developed a profiling tool that computes the important data and the time when these data should be placed into the scratchpad. After this, the application binary is modified in such a way that it adequately configures the MMU and moves the corresponding data into the scratchpad and back, respectively. Because of the static analysis and modification of the application, the points of time at which the scratchpad is accessed are known in advance. Hence, the WCET analysis must be carried out after these modifications for it to deliver a tight result with respect to the scratchpad.

4.2.3. *Instruction scratchpad*

Before a processor executes an instruction, it has to access a memory to fetch this instruction. Hence, an instruction memory is accessed much more often than a data memory and uncertain access times result in a higher inaccuracy of the WCET analysis than an uncertainty of data accesses. Again, the question of which parts of the code should be located inside the scratchpad and which parts should stay in the main memory arises (assuming that not the whole application fits into the scratchpad). Two possibilities using an instruction scratchpad exist.

4.2.3.1. *Static content*

The content of the scratchpad is determined at compile time by profiling. At boot time, selected parts of the code are copied into the scratchpad. Jump and call addresses are already set correctly by the compiler/linker. The advantage of this technique is the static assignment that eases the WCET analysis. Nevertheless, a problem is the profiling: the code parts that turn out to be good candidates because of their frequent execution may not represent the worst-case execution path of the application. Hence, the WCET may not be improved by moving frequently executed parts of the code into the scratchpad.

Instead, code parts with a high impact on the WCET must be selected to be stored in the scratchpad. Unfortunately, moving code parts into the scratchpad, which are responsible for the longest execution path, will shorten this path and another path may get the longest one. To address this problem, multiple iterations of code selection and WCET analysis must be performed in order to have a significant impact on the WCET of an application.

4.2.3.2. *Dynamic content*

Multiple approaches to dynamically change the content of an instruction scratchpad are available in the literature. Most of them are directed toward the optimization of energy consumption, as fetching instructions from the internal memory is much more energy efficient than fetching from an external memory. In general, these approaches are compiler based, i.e. the content of the scratchpad is statically determined by any kind of optimization strategy, and hence they may also be suitable for applications with real-time requirements.

As an example, Egger *et al.* [EGG 06] propose an energy-directed dynamic scratchpad placement strategy based on postpass optimization. Their technique is based on the idea of placing often used code inside the scratchpad. Therefore, they abstract frequently executed loops out of the function code and place them in artificially generated functions. Thereafter, the optimization algorithm classifies each function as one of the following:

SPM: often executed functions are placed statically inside the scratchpad memory (SPM).

Paged: functions that are locally executed very frequently. They are copied into the SPM on demand. From a global point of view, these functions are executed only on a minor number of execution paths.

Ext: functions with a low impact on the energy consumption, i.e. they are executed rarely. They are not copied into the SPM at all.

At runtime, calls to functions of the class Paged are redirected to a special call table. If the function already resides in the scratchpad, a jump to the appropriate target is performed. Otherwise, a so-called *page manager* is called. Its task is to copy the corresponding function into the scratchpad and to update the call table. If necessary, the Page Manager has to evict other function(s).

From the real-time point of view, using the original algorithm to determine the affiliation of the functions to the three classes is problematic. This is because selection of the functions is not based on the worst-case execution path. To improve the real-time behavior of this technique, the algorithm may be changed regarding the following aspects:

– The calls to the paged functions must be highly predictable. This is to correctly estimate the copy overhead and to reduce inaccuracy. The overhead may be accepted as inaccuracy inside the functions may be reduced. This is because fetches from the SPM can be predicted precisely while accesses to the external synchronous dynamic random access memory (SDRAM) may not. In addition, fetches from the scratchpad are much faster than from external memory and hence, data-dependent variations in the number of fetched instructions have a reduced impact on the WCET. The minimum execution time is also decreased for the same reason.

– Functions that will be located in the scratchpad should be selected depending on their internal WCET accuracy. Functions with high accuracy may be located in SPM or Ext, depending on their impact on the WCET. Functions with low accuracy should be executed from the scratchpad in some way. If their calls are predictable, they can be classified as Paged, otherwise they should be statically located in the SPM.

Because measuring the accuracy is not really possible, the WCET of a function must be estimated twice: with execution out of the external memory and with execution out of the scratchpad. Figure 4.11 shows the possible WCET characteristics of EXT, SPM and Paged. The minimum execution time is lowest if the function is executed out of the scratchpad due to the lower fetch latency. In addition, the inaccuracies are lower than using an external RAM, because the timing of the scratchpad is known precisely. Hence, the inaccuracy concerning the fetch accesses is completely eliminated. In contrast, an external dynamic RAM introduces inaccuracy because of unknown situations regarding the refresh and the line buffer. The WCET gain is the sum of the reduced inaccuracies and the improvement of the minimum execution time. If the function is executed only once, the WCET gain must be higher than the time required to copy the function into the scratchpad. If it is called frequently and if it can be guaranteed that it is in the scratchpad's multiple subsequent calls, it is sufficient if the sum of the individual gains is higher than the copy time.

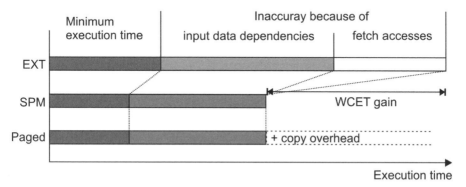

Figure 4.11. *Possible WCET characteristics for EXT, SPM and Paged functions*

Another dynamic scratchpad is presented by Metzlaff *et al.* [MET 08]. Their instruction scratchpad is based on a hardware technique to manage the content. The static code analysis consists only of determining the functions' length. The code itself stays unchanged. This approach dynamically swaps every function into the scratchpad if it requires less than the total amount of SPM. If necessary, another function is evicted. As the scratchpad management is implemented in hardware, no additional call table is necessary. The hardware schematic of the scratchpad is shown in Figure 4.12.

The multiplexer at the fetch bus directs instructions from the scratchpad or from the external memory to the fetch stage of the processor. If the instructions are fetched from the scratchpad, a fetch offset is added to the address. The fetch offset is the shift of the original start address of the currently executed function to their location in the scratchpad. It is determined together with the control signal for the multiplexer at each `call` or `return` instruction that is executed by the processor.

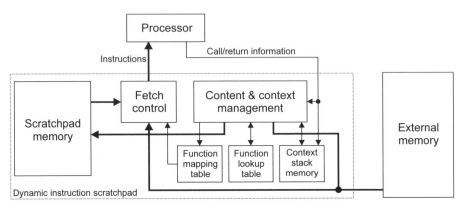

Figure 4.12. *Schematic of a hardware-based dynamic instruction scratchpad*

At the time a `call` or `return` is executed, the target program counter is checked against the start addresses and lengths of all functions that are currently available in the SPM. If the target function is already available, the multiplexer is set to direct fetches to the internal memory and the fetch offset is set appropriately. Otherwise, the control logic determines if the target function should be swapped into the scratchpad. If necessary, several other functions must be evicted using a suitable strategy (e.g. LRU). If the function does not fit completely into the scratchpad, it is executed out of the external memory.

Searching the required function in the scratchpad is based on a translation table memory that allows accesses to multiple table entries in a single cycle. Hence, the parallel accesses also allows parallel comparisons, e.g. if 32 functions can be located in the scratchpad and eight table entries can be read at once, searching a function requires four clock cycles at maximum. Because of the fixed size of the translation table, the total number of instructions located in the scratchpad is restricted by two parameters: the translation table restricts the number of available functions and the memory itself restricts the overall size of the functions.

In general, both approaches, the software-based as well as the hardware-based SPM, can be designed in a way suitable for hard real-time systems. The advantage of the software solution is clearly the smaller hardware effort and its flexibility. But a big disadvantage is the fact that the transfer of instructions into the scratchpad must be done by software, i.e. load accesses to the memory.

Besides the longer time required to copy the instructions, the bigger problem is the data cache pollution if a data cache is available. So, on the one hand, important data may be evicted from the cache and on the other hand, these accesses must be taken into account during the WCET analysis. In contrast, the hardware-based approach uses the fetch data path to load the instructions and has no access to the data cache. In addition, long burst accesses are possible to transfer multiple words at once leading to a shorter transfer time.

4.3. External memories

One of the two main important parts of a computer system is the memory. It is frequently accessed by the processor to fetch instructions and to read and write data. As a result, the time required to access the memory is a dominant fraction of the total execution time of a task. Hence, it is very important to get a tight analysis of the required access times in order to get a significant overall WCET analysis. This chapter outlines several common types of memories and their WCET characteristics.

4.3.1. *Static RAM*

The SRAM is not only the simplest (in terms of its timing behavior) and fastest but also the most expensive type of RAM. The access timing is uniform, i.e. all read accesses and all write accesses follow the same timing. An access is independent of the previous access, if it is of the same type of operation (read or write). In this case, an access is fixed to one or two clock cycles, depending on the clock frequency and the access time of the SRAM.

If reads and writes are mixed up, as is the case for the data memory of general computing systems, the type of the SRAM becomes very important. This is because the direction of the data bus between the memory and the processor has to be changed when issuing a read after a write or a write after a read, respectively. In the following, four types of static memories are described. For simplicity, it is assumed that the internal access time of the memory is less than one clock period unless otherwise noted. Accordingly, the read data are available one cycle after the read address and the read command are issued.

Simple SRAM: a simple SRAM delivers the read data in the clock cycles following the read command and the read address. Multiple subsequent read accesses to different addresses can be issued in a pipelined way. A write access requires the write data and the address in parallel, i.e. in the same bus cycle. If a write has to be performed after a read, a special bus-turnaround cycle is required between reading the read data and sending the write data to avoid bus contention. Hence, the write command must not be sent earlier than two cycles after the read command. On the other hand, if a read follows a write, the latency of the read can be used for turning the bus direction.

Late-write SRAM: the difference of a late-write SRAM and a simple SRAM is the timing of the write access. The read access is unchanged. Writing a value into a late-write SRAM requires the issuing of the write data in the cycles following the write address and write command. Hence, read and write accesses have a symmetrical timing behavior in case of only one latency read cycle. But an additional bus-turnaround cycle is also required to ensure the absence of bus contention. Some late-write SRAMs disable their data output already at the falling edge of the data ready cycle, which would enable the processor to write data immediately after the falling edge. However, at high clock rates, it is difficult to enable the processor's output driver, transmit the write data through the external bus and satisfy the setup time of the SRAM device within a half clock cycle. Asymmetrical timing occurs if more than a single cycle is required for the internal access of the memory. In this case, an additional unused bus cycle arises between a read and a subsequent write access.

Zero bus turn (ZBT) RAM: these types of SRAM are also called *no turnaround (Nt) SRAM* or *no bus latency (NoBL) SRAM*. In contrast to late-write SRAMs, the ZBT SRAMs offer an absolutely identical read/write timing: if the read requires two latency cycles, the write data must also be available two cycles after the write command. In addition, the output drivers of the ZBT SRAM are only active during a short period around the rising clock edge. The processor is allowed to write to the data bus almost directly after the positive clock edge. A special cycle for the change of the bus direction is not required. To ensure proper functionality of the system, absolutely no clock shift between ZBT SRAM and the processor is allowed. Otherwise, the setup and hold times of the registers/latches of the RAM as well as of the processor cannot be satisfied.

Quad data rate (QDR) SRAM: QDR SRAMs implement a completely different strategy than the above-mentioned devices. QDR SRAMs use two independent data busses, one for the write data and the other for the read data. Hence, the timing of reads and writes is also completely independent. Because the address bus and the command lines are commonly used, only one operation (read or write) can be issued in a single cycle. Besides the two busses, QDR devices use the so-called double data rate (DDR) technique to reduce the width of the two data busses. The DDR technique transmits data on every clock edge, e.g. 32 bits of data will be transmitted in two steps within a single clock cycle on a 16 bit bus. Hence, a QDR SRAM requires nearly the same number of I/O pins as other SRAMs with the same data width.

Figure 4.13 demonstrates the different timings of the above-mentioned types of SRAM. It shows a *read, write, read* sequence assuming one cycle internal access time.

Table 4.2 summarizes the worst-case access times of the SRAM types. These values are given in the cases where the memory access sequence is known in advance and where it is unknown, respectively. In addition, the variation between the best-case and the worst-case access times is shown. It is assumed that a processor can issue only a single operation per cycle but it is able to send a write immediately after a read without waiting for the read result (pipelined memory accesses). The presented values include the access request and the acknowledge (write) or data delivery (read) including one cycle bus turnaround, if required. The table is for demonstration purposes only, for authentic values refer to the data sheet of the particular device.

The overview shows that if the access sequence is known, all types of SRAM provide the possibility to calculate a tight WCET analysis statically (with regard to the memory accesses). Unfortunately, the access sequence is difficult to determine in practice. The first problem occurs from the processor itself. If it fetches instructions from the same memory as data are located (*von-Neumann* architecture), fetch accesses and data load and stores are mixed up and they originate from different locations of the processor. Hence, an exact model of the processor is required to predict the access sequence precisely in advance. But even if such a precise model is available, the execution path of a task, and hence the memory access sequence, can depend on input data, which leads to at least some memory accesses with an unknown predecessor. Independent of the processor, external events such as a direct memory access (DMA) transfer or an interrupt request (assuming that both are analyzable and with higher priority than the running task) can occur at any time and, hence, an access sequence analysis is impossible.

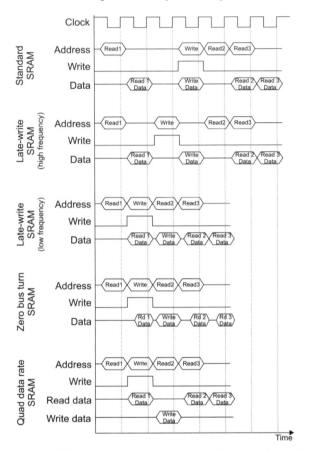

Figure 4.13. *Memory access cycles to a simple SRAM, a late-write SRAM, a ZBT SRAM and a QDR SRAM*

According to the problems with the access sequence analysis, only the late-write SRAM with low frequency, the ZBT SRAM and the QDR SRAM allow an exact prediction of the memory access times. Even if the variations seem to be very low, they accumulate over all memory accesses, and in combination with some techniques described later (caches, branch prediction), their impact on the WCET of the task increases.

	Unknown sequence				Known sequence			
	Access cycles		Variations		Access cycles		Variations	
			(WCET-BCET)				(WCET-BCET)	
Memory	Read	Write	Read	Write	Read	Write	Read	Write
Simple SRAM	2	3	0	2	2	1,3	0	0
Late-write SRAM								
Low frequency	2	1	0	0	2	1	0	0
High frequency	3	2	1	1	2,3	1,2	0	0
ZBT SRAM	2	1	0	0	2	1	0	0
QDR SRAM	2	1	0	0	2	1	0	0

Table 4.2. *Overview of some timing parameters of different types of SRAM*

4.3.2. *Dynamic RAM*

Dynamic RAM offers a higher storage density than SRAM in parallel to a lesser cost. As a result, dynamic RAM is preferred for commercial devices, whose development is cost-pressure driven. The reason for the higher density is a much simpler design of single memory cell. Dynamic RAM uses a kind of small capacitor to store the information of a single bit while an SRAM cell requires six transistors. The drawback of the dynamic RAM technology is that the capacitors need periodic refresh cycles to ensure that their state is not lost by self-discharge. In Addition, the data stored inside the capacitors can be read only once. After a read, the data have to be rewritten into the capacitors again.

The general layout of a dynamic RAM is shown in Figure 4.14. The memory is organized in several banks (typically four banks) and each bank comprises a nearly quadratic matrix of memory cells. To access a byte of the memory, the corresponding row has to be copied completely into the row buffer outside the matrix. The row buffer itself is based on static memory cells. In a second step, the required data can be read out from the row buffer or new values can be stored inside it. When the data of the selected row are no longer required, these have to be written back (*precharged*) into the matrix.

Most dynamic RAMs support two kinds of precharge mode: explicit or automatic precharge. In automatic precharge mode, the row buffer is written back automatically after each access, while in explicit mode, it is not. Filling the row buffer and reading out as well as writing the data into the buffer must be done by explicit commands. Therefore, the memory device offers an address bus, a bidirectional data bus and several control signals. The commands, e.g. *row select*, *column select* or *precharge*, are represented by special signal combinations at the control signals. If required, an address is given by the address bus for row or column selection. In the case where the memory device supports multiple banks, the target bank address is also given on the address bus. Figure 4.15 shows a typical read access followed by a write. The NOP commands are required to finish the auto-precharge assumed in this figure. Depending on the clock frequency, a different number of $NOPs$ could be required and also several $NOPs$ between the $RowSelect$ and the $Read/Write$ commands can be necessary.

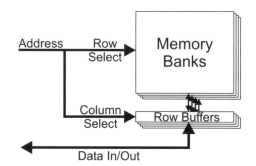

Figure 4.14. *Principal layout of a dynamic RAM*

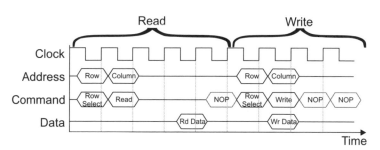

Figure 4.15. *Typical read/write accesses to a dynamic RAM with auto-precharge. The* NOP *operations provide the time required to finish the precharge*

Independent from the explicit data accesses, each row has to be read out and rewritten periodically to perform a refresh of the data stored in the dynamic memory cells. These refresh cycles require the same hardware infrastructure as the ordinary memory accesses and must also be initiated by the external memory controller. A special *refresh* command must be applied to the control signals to initiate a refresh action. A single refresh generally requires four clock cycles and may affect a single row in only one bank or in all banks simultaneously.

Because of the complex actions required for memory access, dynamic RAM has no homogeneous timing behavior like SRAM. Besides the sequence of read and write accesses, the following two factors also influence the timing of a memory access.

Time of access: the refresh cycles have to be performed within predefined periods. If an access is required at the same time a refresh cycle has to be executed, the memory access has to be delayed. Otherwise, data integrity cannot be guaranteed. Because a refresh requires four clock cycles and can collide with every memory access, a pessimistic WCET analysis must take these four cycles into account at any memory access. But, due to the fixed period of refresh cycles, it can be guaranteed that if a certain memory access collides with a refresh, the accesses immediately following the first access will not collide.

Location of data: if the required memory cell is located in the same row as the previously accessed cell, it is already present in the row buffer. Hence, it is not required to transfer the row into the buffer again (if auto-precharge is disabled).

At first glance, WCET analysis support by the compiler/linker could improve the WCET tool's knowledge of memory locations and would theoretically allow for a more thorough analysis. Unfortunately, a refresh cycle requires that the row buffer is overrided by the row that has to be refreshed. As a result, the content of the row buffer cannot be reliably determined by the WCET tool in all cases even if the location of subsequent accesses is known. But, due to the period of typically approximately 16 ms between two refresh cycles, it is possible to assume a single additional row activation cycle every 16 ms within subsequent accesses to the same row.

In principal, assuming that no access will occur at the same time as a refresh cycle is possible if the time required for the appropriate number of refreshes is taken into account by the static WCET analysis. Unfortunately, the analysis of techniques described in sections 3.1, 3.4 and 4.1.2 requires an exact knowledge of the timing of memory accesses. In this case, the general increase of the WCET is not a suitable approach.

In the case where a single program accesses the memory with no DMA transfers and no interrupts, the following approach allows an almost exact analysis of the access timing. A memory access latency of one clock cycle and no additional cycles between row select and read/write are assumed.

To get rid of the overhead of refresh cycles, a new idea is based on the following three minor modifications:

1) The period between refresh cycles must not be the maximum period. Instead, a new refresh must be scheduled early enough before the maximum period: there must remain enough time for the refresh (approximately four cycles) and for a complete memory access cycle (approximately five cycle).

2) Memory accesses (load/store instructions) should have a distance of a complete refresh cycle (approximately four cycles). Otherwise, artificial NOP instructions should be inserted or the missing cycles have to be added to the accesses' execution time. But in this case, the analysis gets more imprecise.

3) The processor must be able to announce memory accesses to the memory controller one refresh cycle (approximately four clock cycles) minus one clock cycle in advance. Due to the fact that most modern processors are designed in a pipelined way (see section 3.1), the announcement is possible if the distance between the decode stage and the execution stage exceeds the required number of cycles.

Figure 4.16 illustrates the accesses to the memory. No access will ever collide with a memory refresh or the refresh will be delayed in order to offer first priority to the processor.

Obviously, the memory throughput is only slightly higher than half the maximum throughput (of depending read accesses with arbitrary addresses), which could reduce performance. But fortunately, a static analysis of the Java virtual machine (JVM) of the Komodo Java microcontroller described in section 6.1 showed that only 18% of all memory accesses are affected by the minimum access distance. As Figure 4.17 shows, approximately 12% of all memory accesses must be delayed by a single cycle, 4% by two cycles and only 2% by three cycles. The latter are mainly caused by 64 bit accesses that required two memory accesses with the used memory infrastructure. Extending the memory interface to 64 bit would avoid almost all of them.

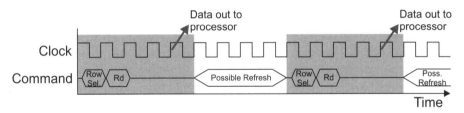

Figure 4.16. *Refresh-independent accesses to dynamic RAM with four cycles access distance*

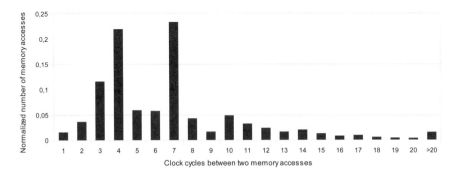

Figure 4.17. *Statically determined clock cycles between two consecutive memory accesses normalized to the total amount of memory accesses. The measurement is based on the JVM of the Komodo microcontroller*

An improvement of the memory throughput can be achieved in two ways, depending on the target and the available hardware. Both approaches can also be used in combination.

Performance of the hard real-time thread is not important: if the performance of the hard real-time task is not the main objective but its predictability and several non- and soft real-time threads are executed in parallel on a multithreaded or multicore processor (see section 3.3 and Chapter 5), the slot between two consecutive hard real-time accesses is suitable for a non- or soft real-time memory access (the distance between two hard real-time accesses has to be increased to five cycles). If a refresh cycle is performed at that time, the non/soft real-time access has to be delayed until the next free slot. It must be mentioned that the non/soft real-time access has to be initiated directly after the preceding hard real-time access. If the succeeding hard real-time access is deferred, it is not allowed to initiate a second non/soft real-time access. Instead of software-based memory accesses, DMA transfers can also be executed in between two hard real-time accesses.

The performance of the hard real-time task is the main objective: refreshes must be controlled by the software. The period between two refresh cycles is given as a maximum period at the specification of the memory device. Hence, it is possible to perform refreshes in much shorter periods. If the WCET analysis tool is aware of the refresh cycles, it is possible to execute memory accesses continuously until the maximum refresh period is reached. A special instruction initiating a refresh cycle must be supported by the processor and the WCET tool has to insert this instruction at appropriate locations into the code, e.g. before a loop subsequently scanning a byte array. In the case where the refresh is not issued by the software/processor, the memory controller has to refresh the memory in time, i.e. the *refresh* instruction can be used optionally by the software to speed up subsequent accesses.

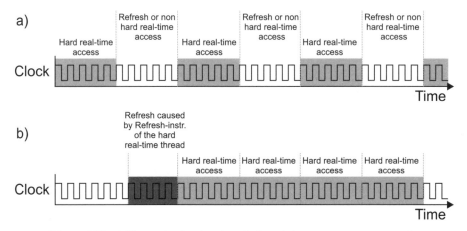

Figure 4.18. *a) Alternating hard and non/soft real-time memory accesses and b) usage of optional* refresh *instructions*

The two approaches are illustrated in Figure 4.18. Remember that the WCET analysis tool should be aware of loop bounds. So, it is possible to determine the time required to execute a complete loop and to place the refresh instructions appropriately. If the WCET of a complete hard real-time task is less than the refresh period (approximately 16 ms), a single *refresh* instruction at the start of the task is sufficient to guarantee the task's execution without any refresh interference.

To speed up the execution of non- and soft real-time threads running in parallel, a supplementary memory access announcement instruction (*MemAnnounce*) can be introduced. This instruction is used to indicate the minimum distance in clock cycles to the next memory access. Thus, the time between two consecutive hard real-time memory accesses can be used to effectively execute multiple non- and soft real-time accesses without any interference to the hard real-time thread. Instead of adding a new instruction, it is also possible to integrate the distance into the coding of the previous memory access instruction. Of course, the memory access announcement can also be applied with SRAM to allow overlapped accesses of hard real-time and non-hard real-time accesses.

Another approach is presented by Edwards *et al.* [EDW 09]. Their memory access pattern is derived from the used processor architecture. The processor supports multiple threads scheduled in an RR way (see section 3.3). The memory access slots are synchronized to the execution slots. The authors assume that each thread accesses its own memory bank. This technique allows the decoupling of the refresh cycles of the banks and guarantees no interferences between the memory accesses of the different threads. The refresh cycles are also, but not explicitly, triggered by the processor, e.g. by a branch instruction, and hence cannot collide with memory access instructions. The RR scheduling allows hard real-time threads in each thread slot. On the other hand, no communication is possible through the memory and the memory throughput is restricted depending on the number of threads. Another drawback is the pure performance of each individual thread that is limited to a fraction of the processor's overall performance (see section 6.3).

4.3.3. *Flash memory*

In contrast to the memories described above, flash memories are non-volatile. In addition, writing to a flash memory is possible only in blocks and requires special actions. Flash memories are organized in blocks of several to hundreds of kilobytes that must be erased at a stretch. Writing is possible in smaller blocks of approximately 16–128 bytes but before a block is written, it must be erased first. Moreover, only a restricted number of erase cycles are allowed with a flash memory, due to the aging of the flash memory cells at each erase action.

Because of the organization of flash memories, they are not suitable as random read and write devices. Nevertheless, flashes are perfectly suitable as instruction memories for embedded systems. They are reprogrammable for software updates and very robust against physical factors such as shocks and heating (compared to a hard drive, for example).

A drawback of using flashes as instruction memories is their long access latency. Reading from an arbitrary address typically requires between 90 and 180 ns, depending on the type of device. Pipelining several read accesses is not possible because the address must remain stable during the complete access. Hence, applying a kind of memory hierarchy as described in section 5 is mandatory. Therefore, modern flash devices support a burst mode that allows us to subsequently read multiple sequential addresses with less read latency [SPA 10]. However, the timing for a single as well as a burst access is exactly known in advance, which simplifies the WCET analysis.

5

Multicores

A multicore processor is a processor chip containing multiple complete processor cores of any type. In particular, it is possible that multiple processors of different types or architectures are integrated in a single chip. Moreover, these processor cores can be single- or multithreaded as well as single- or multi-issue or processor cores. A common feature of multicore processors is the shared main memory used by all processors and, with respect to the real-time capability and the analyzability, it is this shared memory and the corresponding interconnection that are of high interest.

5.1. Impact of resource sharing on time predictability

Multicore processors execute several tasks concurrently to improve the usage of some of the hardware resources by sharing them among tasks (mainly the communication infrastructure and part of the memory hierarchy). Some of these resources (e.g. caches) are referred to as *storage* resources because they keep information for a while, generally for several cycles. On the other hand, *bandwidth* resources (e.g. bus slots) are typically reallocated at each cycle. This terminology is taken from [CAZ 04] where it is used to describe resources in multithreaded processors.

Resource sharing is likely to impact the timing of instructions. For a bandwidth resource, possible conflicts between concurrent tasks to access the resource may delay some of the other tasks. As a result, some instruction latencies are lengthened. In a multicore, the latency of an access to the main memory may be increased because of the waiting time for the bus.

The effects of sharing storage resources are twofold. On the one hand, the resource (e.g. cache) capacity that is usable by a task may be less than that expected since some entries may be occupied by other tasks. On the other hand, shared memories like caches may have their contents corrupted by other tasks, which can prove to be either destructive or constructive. A destructive effect is observed when another task degrades the memory contents from the point of view of the task under analysis: for example, another task replaces a cache line that had been loaded by the analyzed task and is still useful. On the contrary, a constructive effect improves the situation for the task under analysis: for example, a cache line that it requires has been brought into the cache by another task (this may happen when the tasks share parts of code or data). However, even what is seen as constructive in the average case might impair the results of worst-case execution time (WCET) analysis if the processor suffers from timing anomalies [LUN 99b], [REI 06] (in that case, a miss in the cache does not always lead to the WCET).

5.2. Timing analysis for multicores

Three types of approach exist to the problem of accounting for parallel task interferences when computing the WCET of one of these tasks. They differ from each other by the way they consider that the impact of concurrent tasks should be taken into account. In the following, τ represents a task under WCET analysis, while Γ stands for the set of its concurrent tasks.

Joint analysis: this considers the set of tasks altogether in order to determine their possible interactions. As far as storage resources are concerned, this means analyzing the code of each task in $\Gamma \cup \{\tau\}$ to determine possible conflicts, and then accounting for the impact of these conflicts on the WCET of τ. For bandwidth resources, identifying conflicts generally requires considering all the possible task interleavings, which is likely to be complex with fine-grained interleavings (e.g. at instruction or memory access level).

The feasibility of joint analysis techniques relies on all the co-running tasks being known at the time of analysis. This might be an issue when considering a mixed-criticality workload for which non-critical tasks are dynamically scheduled (then any non-critical task in the system should be considered as a potential opponent). In addition, it may happen that the non-critical tasks have not been developed with WCET analysis in mind and they may not be analyzable, e.g. due to tricky control flow patterns. Also, even with a homogeneously critical workload, the set of tasks that may be co-scheduled with the task under analysis depends on the schedule that, in turn, is determined from the tasks' WCETs.

Control of resource sharing: acknowledging the difficulty of analyzing storage and bandwidth conflicts accurately, a number of solutions have been proposed to statically master the task interferences so that they might be more easily taken into account in the WCET analysis. The techniques in this category all require having knowledge of the complete workload.

Controlling interferences in storage resources generally consists of limiting such interferences by restricting accesses to the shared resource. As we will see in the following sections, the proposed techniques of this type do tend to meet the requirements of static WCET analysis techniques in terms of reduced complexity, but the solutions based on static control proposed for bandwidth resources do not fit the principles of static WCET analysis.

Task isolation: the objective is to make it possible to analyze the WCET of a task/thread without any knowledge on the concurrent tasks/threads. This is achieved through the design of hardware schemes that exhibit predictable behavior for shared resources. For storage resources, a common approach is to partition the storage among the tasks, so that each critical task has a private partition. For bandwidth resources, an appropriate arbitration is needed, which guarantees upper bound delays independently of the workload.

5.2.1. *Analysis of temporal/bandwidth sharing*

5.2.1.1. *Joint analysis of conflict delays*

Crowley and Baer considered the case of a network processor running pipelined packet handling software [CRO 03]. The application includes several threads, each one implementing one stage of the computation. The processor features fine-grained multithreading: it provides specific hardware to store the architectural state of several threads, which allows fast context switching, and switches to another thread whenever the current thread is stalled on a long-latency operation. The time during which a thread is suspended depends on the time in which the other threads can execute before, in turn, yielding control so that the first thread can resume its execution. The proposed approach consists of determining the overall WCET of the application (set of concurrent threads) by considering the threads altogether. The control flow graphs (CFGs) used for static WCET analysis are augmented with *yield nodes* at the points where the threads will yield control. *Yield edges* link each yield node of a given thread to all the return-from-yield nodes of any other thread that is likely to be selected when it is suspended. This results in a complex global CFG that, in addition to the control flow of each thread, expresses the possible control flow from one thread to another. From this CFG, an integer linear program is built and used to determine the overall WCET of the application, using the implicit path enumeration technique (IPET) [LI 95a]. Our feeling is that such an approach is not scalable and cannot handle complex applications.

5.2.1.2. *Statically scheduled access to shared bandwidth resources*

To improve the analyzability of latencies to a shared bus in a multicore architecture, Rosén *et al.* [ROS 07] introduce a time division multiple access (TDMA)-based bus arbiter. A *bus schedule* contains a number of slots, each allocated to one core, and is stored in a table in the hardware. At runtime, the arbiter periodically repeats the schedule and grants the bus to the core to which the current slot has been assigned. The idea behind this scheme is that a predefined bus schedule makes the latencies of bus accesses predictable for WCET analysis. This relies on the assumption that it is possible, during the low-level analysis, to determine the start time of each node (basic block) in the CFG so that it can be decided whether an access to the bus is within a bus slot allocated to the core or is to be delayed. This assumption does not hold for static WCET analysis techniques. It would require unrolling all the possible paths in the CFG, which clearly goes against the root principles of static analysis. Moreover, in the case of multiple possible paths (which is the common case), a block is likely to exhibit a large number of possible start times, which will notably complicate the WCET computation. Alternatively, the delay in gaining access to the bus could be upper bounded by the sum of the other slots lengths. This would come down to the simple round-robin solution discussed below if slots are as short as the bus latency, but would probably severely degrade the worst-case performance with longer slots. For these reasons, we believe that static WCET analysis can gain the advantage of static bus scheduling only for applications that exhibit a very limited number of execution paths, as targeted by the single-path programming paradigm [PUS 02].

5.2.1.3. *Task-independent bandwidth partitioning schemes*

Solutions to make the latencies to shared bandwidth resources predictable are possible using bandwidth partitioning techniques. This is what we call *task isolation*: an upper bound of the shared resource latency is known (it does not depend on the nature of the concurrent tasks) and can be considered for WCET analysis.

Mische *et al.* [MIS 10a] introduce CarCore, a multithreaded embedded processor that supports one hard real-time thread (HRT) together with non-critical threads. Temporal thread isolation is ensured for the HRT only, in such a way that its WCET can be computed as if it was executed alone in the processor (i.e. its execution time cannot be impacted by any other thread).

When considering multiple critical threads running simultaneously either in a simultaneous multithreading (SMT) core or in a multicore architecture (with one HRT per core), most of the approaches are based on round-robin-like arbitration, which allows considering an upper bound on the latency to the shared resource: $D = N \times L - 1$, where L is the latency of the resource and N is the number of competing tasks. Barre *et al.* [BAR 08] propose an architecture for an SMT core supporting several critical threads: to provide time-predictability, the storage resources (e.g. instruction queues) are partitioned and the bandwidth resources (e.g. functional units) are scheduled by such a round-robin scheme. Paolieri *et al.* [PAO 09a] propose a round-robin arbiter for the bus to the shared memory hierarchy in a multicore architecture. This scheme is completed by a time-predictable memory controller [PAO 09b] that also guarantees upper bounds on the main memory latencies. Bourgade *et al.* [BOU 10] introduce a multiple-bandwidth bus arbiter where each core is assigned a priority level that defines its upper bound delay to gain access to the bus. This scheme better fits workloads where threads exhibit heterogeneous demands on the main memory.

The MERASA project [UNG 10] funded by the European Community (FP7 program) has designed a complete time-predictable multicore architecture with SMT cores, which implements some of the mechanisms mentioned above.

The PRET architecture [LIC 08] is built around a thread-interleaved pipeline: it includes private storage resources for six threads and each of the six pipeline stages processes an instruction from a different thread. To prevent long-latency instructions from stalling the pipeline and thus impacting the other threads, these instructions are replayed during the thread's slots until completion. Each thread has private instruction and data scratchpad memories and the off-chip memory is accessed through a *memory wheel* scheme where each thread has its own access window.

5.2.2. *Analysis of spatial sharing*

5.2.2.1. *Joint analysis of memories*

Several recent papers focus on the analysis of the possible corruption of L2 shared instruction caches by concurrent tasks [YAN 08, LI 09, HAR 09c]. The general process is as follows: L1 and L2 instruction cache analysis is first performed for each task in $\Gamma \cup \{\tau\}$ independently, ignoring interferences, using usual techniques [FER 99b]; then, the results of the analysis of the L2 cache for task τ are modified considering that each cache set used by another task in T is likely to be corrupted. For a direct-mapped cache, as studied by Yan and Zhang [YAN 08], any access to a conflicting set is classified as ALWAYS_MISS (should be NOT_CLASSIFIED if timing anomalies occur). For a set-associative cache, as considered by Li *et al.* [LI 09] and Hardy *et al.* [HAR 09c], possible conflicts impact the ages of cache lines.

The main concern with this general approach is its scalability to large tasks: if the number of possible concurrent tasks is large and if these tasks span widely over the L2 cache, we expect most of the L2 accesses to be NOT_CLASSIFIED, which may lead to an overwhelmingly overestimated WCET. For this reason, Li *et al.* [LI 09] refine the technique by introducing an analysis of task lifetimes, so that tasks that cannot be executed concurrently (according to the scheduling algorithm, which is non-preemptive and static priority-driven in this paper, and to intertask dependencies) are not considered as possibly conflicting. Their framework involves an iterative worst-case response time analysis process, where each iteration (1) estimates the best-case execution time (BCET) and WCET of each task according to expected conflicts in the L2 cache; (2) determines the possible task schedules, which may show that some tasks cannot overlap (the initial assumption is that all tasks overlap). This approach is likely to reduce pessimism but may not fit independent tasks with a more complex scheduling scheme.

Another solution to the complexity issue has been proposed by Hardy *et al.* [HAR 09c]: they introduce a compiler-directed scheme that enforces L2 cache bypassing for single-usage program blocks. This sensibly reduces the number of possible conflicts. Lesage *et al.* [LES 10] have recently extended this scheme to shared data caches.

5.2.2.2. *Storage partitioning and locking schemes*

Cache partitioning and locking techniques were first proposed as a means to simplify the cache behavior analysis in single-core non-preemptive systems [PUA 02b, PUA 06b, RED 07, PLA 09]. Recently, these techniques have been investigated by Suhendra and Mitra [SUH 08] to assess their usability in the context of shared caches in multicore architectures. They considered combinations of (static or dynamic) locking schemes and (core-based or task-based) partitioning techniques. They discovered that (1) core-based partitioning strategies (where each core has a private partition and any task can use the entire partition of the core on which it is running) outperform task-based algorithms; (2) dynamic locking techniques, which allow reloading the cache during execution, lead to lower WCETs than static approaches.

Paolieri *et al.* [PAO 09a] investigate software-controlled hardware cache partitioning schemes. They consider columnization (each core has a private write access to one or several ways in a set-associative cache) and bankization (each core has a private access to one or several cache banks) techniques. In both cases, the number of ways/banks allocated to each core can be changed by software, but it is assumed to be fixed all along the execution of a given task. They show that bankization leads to tighter WCET estimates.

Techniques to achieve timing predictability in SMT processors are also based on partitioning instruction queues [BAR 08, MIS 10a].

5.3. Local caches

Local caches are very important in multicore systems since they reduce the pressure on the main memory that is accessed by multiple processor cores in parallel. Moreover, in systems with a higher number of cores, a simple bus-based interconnection is no longer possible. Instead, a more complex network on a chip is required to establish the communication with a memory resulting in longer memory latencies. Applying local caches reduces de facto the number of memory accesses, but concerning hard real-time systems this is of no use if the local caches are not time analyzable.

Even though a local cache is private to a core and, hence, is not a shared resource, cache coherence complicates a static timing analysis. Since cache coherence concerns only data caches, instruction caches are not taken into account in this section.

If multiple cores of a multicore system access the same data, it needs to be guaranteed that the cores always access the most recent data. In other words, if a core modifies a shared variable, all other cores must be able to read the new value. If one of the other caches already holds that variable, it needs to be informed of the modification. Otherwise, the corresponding core would read the old value.

5.3.1. *Coherence techniques*

There are three major ways of implementing coherent accesses to shared data: hardware-based, software-based and hybrid techniques. These three ways are briefly described in the following sections.

5.3.1.1. *Hardware-based coherence*

This way of implementing coherent accesses relies only on hardware extensions and no software support is required. Hence, coherence is maintained at all times for all data without any exception, i.e. these techniques implement strong consistency. Hardware-based techniques can be classified in two categories:

1) Snooping-based coherence techniques: these techniques are used in systems with a small number of cores (two to eight) that are connected by a common bus to a shared memory. During an operation, all cores listen to the bus activities of the other cores. Additionally, activities that may influence the cache content of other cores are indicated by coherence messages on the bus. If a core recognizes that another core wants to read recently modified data, actions are triggered to keep the access coherent, e.g. by interrupting the actual bus transfer and writing modified data back into the memory.

Many different snooping-based protocols have been introduced and can be classified into *write-invalidate* [KAT 85a] [KAT 85b] [PAP 84] and *write-update* protocols [THA 87]. Comprehensive performance analyses on these approaches have been made by Tomasevic [TOM 94] and Stenstrom [STE 90].

Popular implementations of snooping-based coherence techniques are the MESI and the MOESI protocols. In both cases, each cache line is extended by a state that indicates if the corresponding data are *modified* locally, *exclusively* available in the local cache, *shared* unmodified with other caches or *invalid*. The MOESI protocol also supports the state *owned*, which simplifies cache-to-cache communication.

2) Directory-based coherence techniques: in contrast to snooping-based techniques, the cores in directory-based systems do not need to check every action performed by other cores. Instead, a more or less central instance is aware of read and write accesses to different memory regions and, hence, it is possible to guarantee coherent accesses to shared data. Directory-based techniques are used for systems comprising large numbers of cores, including large-scale shared memory multiprocessors, since communication distances result only in a performance reduction but coherence can still be granted.

Directory-based coherence protocols can be classified into *full-map directory schemes* [MAA 91] [O'KR 90] holding a centralized directory in the main memory. To reduce the memory overhead of full-map directories, *limited* [AGA 88] and *chained directory schemes* [THA 90] have been proposed. As optimization, some techniques use the operating system to distinguish between private and shared memory blocks [CUE 11, HAR 09a, HAR 09b] or to perform region tracking [JER 08, ZEB 07].

5.3.1.2. *Software-based coherence*

Several multi- and many-core systems such as the Intel *single-chip cloud computer* (SCC) do not support hardware cache coherence at all. Instead, additional instructions are available that allow selected cache lines, sets or the complete cache to be invalidated. Nevertheless, these techniques are classified as software based because the major complexity is based on software.

The main reason for omitting cache coherence is the high hardware overhead. The SCC, for example, provides special small message passing memories that allow intercore communication. Accesses to these buffers are not cached in principle and hence data can be accessed coherently.

A method to provide coherent accesses to the main memory is based on the virtual memory management functionalities of the cores [ZHO 10]. Hereby, the states of cache lines used by the hardware-based techniques are mapped to complete virtual memory pages. All changes of state with the corresponding actions are performed by trap routines. Since the complete technique is implemented in software, it brings a notable performance drawback. Moreover, a powerful virtual memory management is not available in most embedded architectures targeting hard real-time systems. Similar techniques are presented by Park *et al.* [PAR 11].

Another solution is to access shared data without caching. This means that special instructions need to be provided by the processor cores or that shared data are stored in non-cacheable memory areas. With this technique, all accesses to shared data have to traverse the interconnection in from the core to the memory, resulting in long latencies. This technique may be efficient with small amounts of shared data but with bigger ones, and in combination with large distances, in the case of many cores, it is not an option. Other approaches are based on the idea of assigning *cacheable* and *non-cacheable* attributes to memory accesses, supported by a compiler analysis [CHE 92]. These methods require additional hardware support to mark cache lines and invalidate cache regions using special invalidation instructions. Some approaches rely on local knowledge using clocks and timestamps to invalidate cache-lines with possibly modified data [DAR 93, MIN 92]. Molnos *et al.* [MOL 06] propose a partitioning scheme where cache sets can be assigned to several tasks or stated for shared use. Due to focussing on throughput optimization, time predictable behavior for hard real-time systems has not been examined.

5.3.1.3. *Hybrid techniques*

There are also hybrid techniques available like the one presented by Kelm *et al.* [KEL 10] which allows dynamic selection between hardware- and software-based coherence. This technique targets reducing coherence messages and hardware overhead, but it also suffers from the lack of analyzability as described in the next section.

Another hybrid approach is the lock-based coherence protocol in JIAJIA [ESK 99]. While using locked critical sections to synchronize accesses to shared data, the protocol still generates coherence transactions between the processing cores to notify modified cache lines, causing unpredictable timing behavior. A similar approach is presented by Ros and Kaxiras [ROS 12], where the classification of private and shared data is based on the used memory page. Since the type of a page is determined dynamically depending on the accessing cores, a complex process is required for the transition of a page from private to shared. Even though no coherence messages are required, the mentioned transition process impedes a tight timing analysis.

To the best of our knowledge, there is no data cache coherence mechanism that aims at real-time capability. Nevertheless, there are several approaches targeting the improvement of memory performance for real-time systems, which should be mentioned. Improvements regarding the timing predictability of memory architectures were introduced, e.g. by Liu *et al.* [LIU 10], relying on scratchpad memories instead of a cache. Concerning real-time capability, some research has been done for instruction caches. By locking and partitioning separate cache areas, the predictability of the cache content could be raised [ASA 07].

5.3.2. *Discussion on timing analyzability*

All well-known coherence techniques focus on optimizing average performance. Timing analyzability is not the focus and so these techniques do not provide a predictable timing behavior. Additionally, static cache state analysis is harmed in most cases. Even though most of the topics discussed in the following sections concern snooping – as well as directory-based approaches – the focus is on snooping-based systems with hardware-supported coherence.

For a tight WCET estimation, a sufficient knowledge of the cache content is required as well as defined latencies for cache hits and misses. The possibility of modifications triggered by other cores prevents it from statically predicting if data are stored in a cache line at a specific point in time. Moreover, the access latencies of caches are no longer predictable, depending on the type of coherence technique. In this connection, it must be differentiated between the two ways of maintaining the coherent access itself:

– *Invalidation*: in case a core wants to write on data present in another local cache, the data in the other cache are invalidated (by hardware or software).

Afterward, a reload of new data is required since an access to that data leads to a cache miss.

– *Update*: if data are present in multiple local caches and modified by one core, the modification is sent to all other cores. Hence, an access to that data by one of the other cores holding that data is still a hit and leads to the current values. Note that this technique requires a write-through policy in order to track all writes in time.

Moreover, the source of data in case of a miss needs to be taken into account. Pure snooping protocols read data from the memory, which requires a write back from another cache if data have been modified. If a bus-snarfing technique is used, the requested data are sent directly from another cache holding that data.

The following four issues demonstrate uncertainties and possible interferences between caches leading to unpredictable modifications of cache content and state as well as mutated timing behavior. Using improper coherence techniques will reduce the tightness of a static timing analysis dramatically and the decision for using a multicore could be at least questionable.

1) Validity of cached data

In coherence techniques using external invalidations, the lifetime of a specific cache line is difficult to predict.

In the case of an invalidation-based technique, a cache line containing data that are shared with other cores can become invalid if another core intends to write on that data.

Even though the lifetime of any private cache line is not directly affected by shared data, the state of the replacement policy can be modified by invalidations of shared cache lines. Of course, this is only valid for associative caches.

Assume a two-way set-associative cache with least recently used (LRU) replacement strategy and the cache line access order A, X, B, A, where the cache lines A and B hold private data and X shared data. All accesses concern the same set. If X is invalidated before the access to B, the free blockframe can be used for B. In the case X is not invalidated, B will evict A and the next access to A will lead to a cache miss. Figure 5.1 shows three scenarios where

(a) and (b) lead to a cache miss at the second access to private variable A while (c) maintains A.

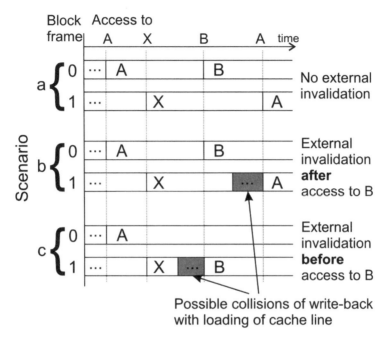

Figure 5.1. *Different scenarios of shared data invalidation can lead to eviction of private data*

As a result, the lifetime of any cache line in an associative cache can be influenced by unpredictable invalidations of other cores. This makes the prediction of the cache's content practically impossible.

Nevertheless, direct-mapped caches do not show the problem of unpredictable replacement status and can be candidates to be used in hard real-time multicore systems, or alternatively modified replacement strategies, which do not change the replacement status in case of an external invalidation, can be implemented. However, cache lines with shared data can be invalidated anyway. Update-based systems do not exhibit these problems.

2) Latency of cache misses while accessing shared data

A cache miss of shared data typically generates a read burst from the main memory. Since data in the main memory could be outdated and the modified data could be present in another core's cache, a previous write back of the cache possessing the data is necessary. This topic is relevant only for write-back policy or if a write buffer is integrated. If a simple write-through write policy (i.e. no write buffers) is applied, this problem does not occur.

The issue of data write back leads to two questions concerning static timing analysis:

a) Is the data required by the local core modified by another (remote) core and not yet written back to the memory?

b) If this is the case, when will the other core be able to react on the request and, if necessary, write back the current data?

Both problems can be addressed by bus interconnects with a slot-based arbitration scheme such as round-robin or TDMA. In both cases, the remote core can use the slot of the local core to react on the read request. This is possible because at that time the remote core is not allowed to perform its own request anyway. Figure 5.2 shows an example timing of a TDMA-based quad-core system in combination with bus-snooping and bus-snarfing technique, respectively.

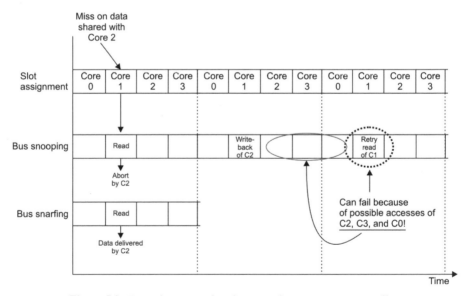

Figure 5.2. *Example timing of cache miss when accessing externally modified shared data. An unpredictable waiting time can occur in case of a bus-snooping technique*

As can be seen in the figure, a snooping-based technique does not meet the requirements of hard real-time systems: In the first step, a core (core 1) issues a read request for a cache line present in another core (core 2). Core 2 has to write back the data first, which cannot be performed in the current time slot because this slot is already occupied by the read request that will be aborted by core 2. Since it is not allowed for core 2 to use its own slot (which is reserved for core 2's memory accesses), the write back has to take place during the next slot of core 1. After that point in time, there is no valid copy of that data in any local cache. This means that any core can access that particular data in the following slots, resulting in the original starting situation from core 1's point of view. In this case, the next trial of core 1 to read the data will fail again. The access latency to shared data (or even a shared cache line) cannot be bounded if a snooping-based technique is used.

With bus snarfing, the data required by core 1 are delivered by core 2 directly, given that core 2 is able to handle the request immediately. Since the read is now an atomic action, it cannot be interrupted or harmed by any other core. The latency of a cache miss can be bound independently from the availability of the corresponding data in other caches.

3) Latency of cache misses while shared data are held by the cache

The latency of any cache miss can be influenced by another core. If a core is holding a modified shared cache line, it can be forced to deliver that cache line to another core. This intervention can delay a local cache miss, resulting in an unpredictable miss latency. One possible solution is to implement the cache as a dual-ported cache resulting in higher hardware complexity or to use a write-through invalidation-based policy.

4) Latency of cache hits on writes

Assume that a core wants to write on a cache line that is already present in the local cache. If this cache line is also available in other cores (i.e. in *shared* state of a MESI protocol if multiple cores read data from the same line), the write cannot be executed immediately.

Figure 5.3 demonstrates the following situation: the local caches of two cores hold the same cache line and both cores want to write on that line in the same cycle. Both cores recognize a hit, which means that each core has to announce the write to the other cores in order to get the line in an *exclusive* state. In a high-performance system, both cores will compete for the bus. The winner will perform the write first and the second core will follow. Unfortunately, this type of bus arbitration is not suitable for hard real-time systems as discussed in section 5.2.1.2.

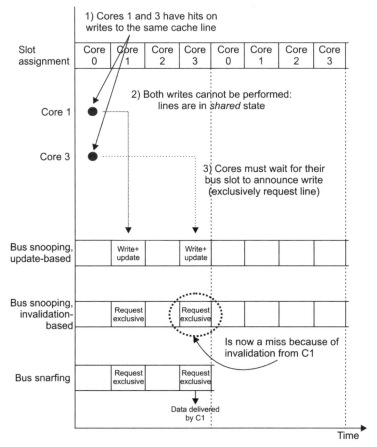

Figure 5.3. *Two cores perform writes to the same cache line that is present in both caches*

In case of a TDMA- or round-robin-based bus arbitration scheme, each core has to wait until its own time slot has arrived before making the announcement. This means that in the worst case, a core has to wait for one TDMA period before performing a write on a cache hit. And this is valid only for a bus-snarfing technique. For bus snooping, a similar situation as described in point (2) can occur, resulting in an unbounded delay.

5.4. Conclusion

Figure 5.4 shows a summary of the problems concerning the time predictability of conventional high-performance coherence techniques. The figure shows direct-mapped caches; if an associative cache is used, the problem of external modifications of the replacement state occurs for all combinations of the shown sub-techniques. The combinations *update* and *write back* are less useful and not taken into account here. The numbers refer to the issues mentioned in the preceding sections, except for *(5)*, which represents the unbounded delay on a write hit (explained in point (4)).

The snooping-based write-back, write-invalidate technique is probably the one most often implemented in general purpose and high-performance systems. As can be seen, this technique suffers from all the above-mentioned issues complicating or impeding a static WCET analysis. In contrast, an update-based bus-snarfing direct-mapped cache with write-through policy can allow a tight static WCET analysis if it is implemented as a dual-ported cache.

While (2) and (4) are important only directly at accesses to shared data, (1) and (3) are relevant at any time after an access to shared data. This is because it is not known when, or even if at all, a cache line with shared data will be accessed by another core. Note that in this case, *shared data* mean cache lines containing data used by multiple core, the concerned data portion is not necessarily the identical one.

5.5. Time-predictable architectures

As shown in the previous section, using a well-known cache coherence protocol in hard real-time systems is not the first choice. Other techniques are required to allow coherent access to shared data and a tight static WCET analysis in parallel.

5.5.1. *Uncached accesses to shared data*

The common straightforward technique is to avoid caching of shared data. This approach guarantees that the data in memory are always up-to-date and that no outdated data are available in local caches. There are two principal ways to implement this technique:

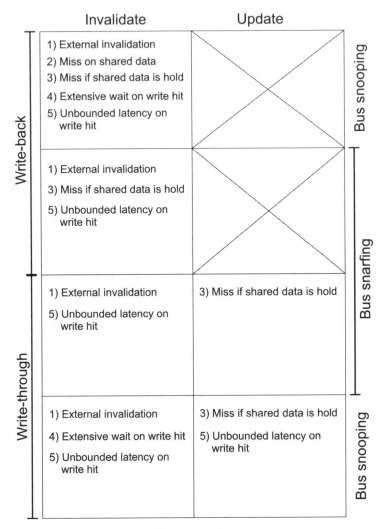

Figure 5.4. *Timing analysis issues of different combinations of cache characteristics*

 – *Instruction set extension*: additional instructions allow uncached accesses to any memory location. Alternatively, a single additional operation instructs the processor to perform the next memory accesses without using the cache. This technique allows us to use shared data in any location of the memory at the cost of an instruction set architecture (ISA) extension.

– *Shared data in a predefined memory location*: a special memory region is excluded from being cached. An ISA modification is not required but shared data are allowed only to be located in that memory region. Alternatively, if the address space is large enough, the main memory can be mapped into two address ranges: accesses through one region use the cache, while accesses through the other do not. With this technique, shared data can be distributed all over the memory.

A clear disadvantage of not caching shared data is that the applications cannot profit from temporal and spatial locality since each access to shared data results in a memory access. If a TDMA-based bus arbitration is applied, a full TDMA period needs to be assumed as waiting time to gain a bus grant during static WCET analysis for each access to shared data. In case of larger sets of shared data, this is a clear disadvantage.

5.5.2. *On-demand coherent cache*

The on-demand coherent cache (ODC^2) allows analyzable caching of private as well as shared data; the latter restricted to special code regions. Within these code regions, it must be guaranteed that only a single core has exclusive access to the corresponding shared data. Mutexes, semaphores or barriers can be used to guarantee that exclusive access. Note that the access to lock and barrier variables is not supported by ODC^2. Instead, dedicated synchronization hardware or uncached accesses as described in the previous section can be used to support these types of variables.

The basic idea of the ODC^2 is to hold shared data only as long as necessary and to force (re-)loading of possibly modified shared data at the time of use. Hereby, *use* does not mean individual accesses but rather instruction sequences that access shared data. The ODC^2 maintains coherent memory accesses only if accesses to shared data are intended, otherwise no coherence is implemented.

To identify instruction sequences that access shared data, the ODC^2 relies on critical sections (protected by mutexes or semaphores) that are in any case required to ensure consistent accesses to (portions of) shared data. Also, barriers are a suitable technique to guarantee exclusive access to (portions of) shared data and can be used with ODC^2.

An application using ODC^2 can take full advantage of caching (private) data in all code sections where no shared data are accessed. Therefore, ODC^2 supports two different working modes: the *normal mode* and the *shared mode*. In normal mode, the ODC^2 acts as a standard cache controller without any coherence functionality since in this mode, no accesses to shared data are allowed. This mode is used as long as the processor has not entered a critical section.

At the time a critical section is entered, the shared mode is activated and the ODC^2 shows additional functionality. Hereby, additional information inside a block frame (see Figure 5.5) is used. If a cache miss occurs, the loaded cache line is marked as shared by the *shared* bit. This bit identifies the cache line as a potential carrier of shared data on which coherence actions are required.

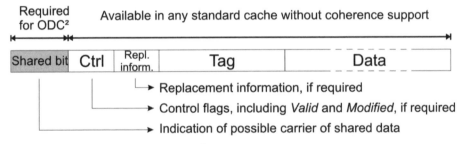

Figure 5.5. *Block frame of ODC^2 including the* shared bit *that tags the block frame to be a possible carrier of shared data*

During *shared mode*, all memory accesses are treated in the described way. At the time of deactivation of *shared mode*, all subsequent memory accesses are stalled and the cache controller performs a *restore procedure*. In case of a *write-back* write strategy, all cache lines marked as *shared* and *modified* are written back to the main memory. In case of a *write-through* policy, no additional write-back is required. Independent from the write policy, all cache lines marked as *shared* are invalidated. After this operation, all shared data are flushed to the main memory and no shared data remain in the cache. Hence, at the next access to the same shared data, it needs to be reloaded from the memory. Thus, shared data accessed by one processor are always consistent with the data accessed by other processors.

The activation and deactivation of the *shared mode* can be triggered either by additional instructions or by accesses to control registers. The former requires an extension of the processor's instruction set. The latter is a less expensive way and uses load and store instructions to specific memory locations. These accesses address the ODC^2 cache controller and set the operation to the required state. The code snippet shown in Figure 5.6 shows an example of a critical section containing the control operations *enter_shared_mode()* and *exit_shared_mode()*. Since these operations are directly related to the beginning and the end of the critical section, they can also be integrated in the *lock()* and *unlock()* functions of the system.

```
.. -- Accesses to private data only -- ..
lock(criticalsection); entersharedmode(); .. -- Accesses to shared
data -- .. exitsharedmode(); unlock(criticalsection); .. -- Accesses
to private data only -- ..
```

Figure 5.6. *Example code snippet with switching ODC^2 mode inside a critical section*

Since data are handled on the granularity of cache lines by the ODC^2, a cache line must not contain shared and private data in parallel. To comply with this requirement, it is sufficient to force an alignment of private/shared data with respect to the size of the cache line.

Using the time-predictable ODC^2 cache, any external modification of cached data and cache state is prohibited. Since no simultaneous accesses of multiple cores to the same shared data emerge and the shared data do not remain in any core's cache after it has been accessed, the four scenarios described in section 5.3.2 cannot appear. Time predictability is essentially improved by ODC^2 at the cost of forced synchronization and alignment of shared data.

6

Example Architectures

In this chapter, seven example processor architectures that implement several of the techniques presented in Chapters 3, 4, and 5, are described. In sections 6.1 to 6.4 single-core processors are discussed, some of these are multithreaded cores. Sections 6.5 to 6.7 focus on multicore architectures for hard real-time systems.

6.1. The multithreaded processor *Komodo*

The *Komodo* processor core executes Java applications natively, i.e. the Java *bytecode* instructions are executed by the processor directly. This means that no additional software layer is required between the Java application and the processor core such as an operating system or a software Java virtual machine (JVM). This circumstance itself dramatically increases the real-time capability and predictability of a Java system. If a JVM and an operating system is applied, these systems must be analyzed together with the application and the processor, resulting in a higher inaccuracy of a static analysis.

Other Java processors, especially for embedded systems, are the SHAP processor [ZAB 09] from University of Dresden, the aJile [AJI 00] from aJile Systems Inc., the PicoJava [HAN 99] from Sun Microsystems (now Oracle Corporation) and the Java Optimized Processor (JOP, see section 6.2).

The decision to develop a multithreaded Java core was based on the idea of handling multiple events simultaneously. The so-called interrupt service threads are responsible for the event handling. In contrast to standard interrupt-based event handling, which is only able to process one event at a time, service threads are executed in an overlapped parallel way in the hardware thread slots of a multithreaded processor. Hence, multiple different events can be handled, each one by its own service thread in its own thread slot. Of course, the number of simultaneously handled events is restricted by the number of hardware thread slots.

Assuming that the handled events must fulfill real-time requirements, the execution of the hardware threads must be scheduled in a real-time capable way. Hence, one of the key features of the *Komodo* processor core is the integrated real-time scheduling. The following sections describe the basic *Komodo* architecture as well as the integrated scheduling techniques.

In addition to the simultaneous event handling, the multithreaded architecture of *Komodo* allows the implementation of a special real-time capable garbage collection. The garbage collection is executed within its own hardware thread slot in parallel to the application threads. Hence, no stop-the-world behavior as known from other garbage collection techniques occurs. A detailed description of the parallel *Komodo* garbage collection is presented by Fuhrmann and Pfeffer [FUH 01].

6.1.1. *The Komodo architecture*

The processor core (see Figure 6.1) contains a multithreaded five-stage pipeline (*instruction fetch, instruction decode, operand fetch, execute* and the *stack cache*) [UHR 07a]. The integrated *real-time scheduler* (priority manager) shown in the figure is responsible for a real-time capable thread schedule if the core is used in real-time applications.

Most of the Java integer as well as several long, float and double bytecodes are executed directly in hardware, mostly within a single execution cycle. Instructions with medium complexity are implemented by microcodes and the complex operations, such as *new, athrow, monitorenter* and most floating point instructions, call trap routines. As operand stack, a 2k-entry stack cache is integrated within the pipeline that is shared between the hardware thread slots. During the initialization phase, different portions of the stack cache can be assigned to the thread slots so that one thread works entirely in the stack cache while the data of other threads have to be swapped in and out. As an example, the garbage collection should run without swapping due to a continuous progress without any additional and avoidable memory accesses for swapping. Because of the required predictability, real-time threads should also run without swapping.

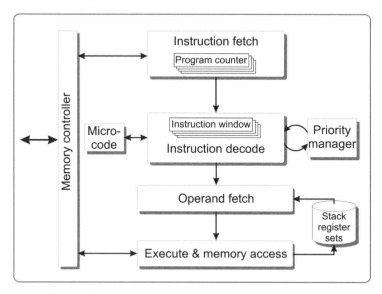

Figure 6.1. *Block diagram of the multithreaded* Komodo *core*

Each thread slot possesses an instruction window (IW) into which up to six bytecodes can be prefetched. These IWs decouple the fetching and decoding of the bytecodes.

While the fetch process is driven by the fill level of the IWs, the decoding is triggered by a real-time scheduling scheme that delivers a scheduling decision on a cycle-by-cycle basis. The backend of the pipeline is designed in a way that allows context switches in the granularity of clock cycles. The execution of microcodes in particular requires the replication of the microcode sequence counter. In addition, all internal pipeline status indicators such as the overflow bit of the execution unit are replicated.

Memory accesses are executed by the *Komodo* research prototype with a higher clock frequency for the memory than for the pipeline. This technique enables the pipeline to access the memory in a single pipeline cycle leading to an exactly predictable access timing. In addition, memory accesses from different threads cannot compete for the memory. The factor of the overclocking depends on the type of memory that is applied: if a static random access memory (RAM) is used, a factor of two is sufficient; applying a dynamic RAM requires a higher factor.

Evaluations [KRE 00a] have shown that the competition of instruction fetches and data memory accesses is not an issue. Because of the data bus width of 32 bit and an average Java bytecode size of 1.8 byte, the IWs always contain enough bytecodes to provide input data for the pipeline backend. Hence, data accesses from the pipeline, which are preferred by the memory interface, do not disrupt the instruction flow.

6.1.2. *Integrated thread scheduling*

The real-time scheduler integrated in the *Komodo* processor core supports four scheduling schemes. One of the scheduling schemes can be selected for the operation mode. The scheduling is responsible to select the thread slot/IW from which the next instruction is taken from. It is completely decoupled from the instruction fetch, which is based only on the fill level of the IWs. Of course, the fetch strategy indirectly depends on the scheduling decision because the thread that is executed most often has the least number of instructions in its IW. The implemented scheduling schemes are as follows:

– *Fixed priority pre-emptive (FPP)*: the FPP is the most simple scheduling within the *Komodo*. Using FPP, a fixed priority is assigned to each thread slot. The priority is in the range of 0 to $\#number\_of\_slots - 1$, where 0 exhibits the highest priority. The currently active thread with the highest priority is selected for execution.

– *Earliest deadline first (EDF)*: EDF is a very powerful real-time scheduling scheme. The *Komodo* scheduler requires a 32 bit value per thread slot representing the deadline. The deadlines are given relatively in units of pipeline clock cycles. For execution, the currently active thread with the lowest deadline value is executed. All deadline values are decremented in each clock cycle.

– *Least laxity first (LLF)*: even though two values per thread are required for LLF scheduling (the deadline and the worst-case execution time (WCET) of each thread), the *Komodo* scheduler only requires a single value per thread: the laxity, which is equal to $deadline - WCET$. The currently active thread with the least laxity is selected for execution. The laxity values of all threads that are not executed in the actual cycle are decremented. Hereby, threads with current latencies are also counted as executed.

– *Guaranteed percentage (GP)*: the GP [KRE 00b] scheduling was especially developed for multithreaded processors with a zero cycle context switch overhead. It is described in section 6.1.3.

The presented scheduling schemes must be selected statically, i.e. before the *Komodo* processor starts operation, the scheduling type as well as the parameters must be set.

6.1.3. *Guaranteed percentage scheduling*

The GP scheduling scheme assigns each thread a specific percentage of the processor's performance over a short period of 100 processor cycles. In case of three threads A, B and C, we may assign 20% of the processor performance to thread A, 30% to thread B and 50% to thread C. The scheduler takes care that each thread gets an appropriate amount of computing performance and that the latency cycles of one thread are filled by the execution of another thread (see Figure 6.2). The fixed percentages of GP allow a steady progress of the threads.

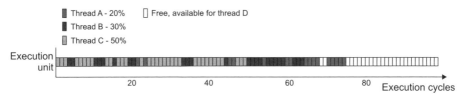

Figure 6.2. *Example execution of GP scheduled threads within an interval of 100 clock cycles*

The GP scheduler of the *Komodo* processor offers three classes describing how a requested percentage is assigned to a thread:

– *Exact:* a thread gets exactly the requested percentage of the processor's performance in the interval, not more and not less. This mode is very useful, if a thread has to keep a specific data rate, e.g. while reading or writing data to an interface with a low jitter. Also deadlines can be met if the percentage is selected depending on the WCET and the deadline.

– *Minimum:* a thread gets at least the requested percentage of the processor's performance in the interval. If additional execution cycles are left in the interval, the thread may receive more. This mode is useful if a minimum processing performance is required. For example, the garbage collection can be executed with a minimum throughput but if the processor offers more free execution cycles, these cycles can be used by the garbage collection.

– *Maximum:* if a thread is present that has to perform some minor important work, it can be scheduled using the *maximum* scheduling. In this case, the thread is executed at each free execution cycle as long as its maximum number of execution cycles is not reached.

Threads of different classes may be mixed within a single processor the workload. A special Java class supports the handling of the hardware thread slots and the GP scheduling policies after a GP is selected statically as the scheduling algorithm.

A workload with GP threads must not exceed the 100% processor performance that can be statically assigned. Nevertheless, the existence of latency cycles, which are filled by the multithreading technique, allows a dynamic utilization of more than 100% used by threads of the class *minimum*.

In the context of very fast context switching, the quality of latency utilization strongly depends on the number of threads waiting for execution. The processor needs a pool of these threads to switch in case of a latency. If there are not enough threads active, the processor may not find an appropriate thread to execute. Standard real-time scheduling schemes such as EDF or FPP tend to lessen this pool, because they first execute the most important thread, then the second most important thread, etc. [KRE 00b]. In contrast, the GP scheduling as well as LLF tend to keep threads alive as long as possible. So, GP and LLF allow a very efficient utilization of a multithreaded processor.

6.1.4. *The jamuth IP core*

Starting from the multithreaded *Komodo* research microcontroller, an IP core for Altera FPGAs was developed [UHR 08, UHR 07b]. The IP core is called Java multithreaded *jamuth* and can be used for any Altera FPGA by Altera's so-called SOPC-Builder.

The IP core contains three additional units: the *Evaluation unit*, the *Java timer* and an *Interrupt controller* (IRQ controller). The first unit is responsible for debug and observing functionalities, the timer is required for the JVM (*System.currentTimeMillis*) and the *Sleep* methods) and the IRQ controller translates interrupt requests from the peripheral components to wake-up signals for the thread slots or interrupt signals, respectively, for already running threads.

In addition, the memory interface was changed in a way that the *jamuth* can be connected to any memory device by an appropriate memory controller. The connection between the *jamuth* and the memory controller is established by an Avalon interconnect, a standard interconnect for Altera FPGAs. Two master 64 bit bus interfaces for memory accesses are available: one for instruction fetching and one for data accesses. Besides the memory interfaces, a 32 bit peripheral interface is also present, which is equipped with interrupt request inputs.

Because of the changed memory interface, memory accesses can no longer be performed in a single processor cycle. To reduce the pressure on the memory controller, instructions can now be fetched from three different sources: external memory, instruction cache and scratchpad RAM. Threads with hard real-time requirements as well as garbage collection should be located inside the scratchpad. The reasons are different: while hard real-time threads require a predictable fetch of instructions (which can be guaranteed by the scratchpad), the garbage collection should use the scratchpad to reduce its impact on the other thread. Executing the garbage collection with GP scheduling out of the external memory by using the cache would cache pollute the instruction cache continuously.

The last change concerns the internal thread scheduler. Its scheduling algorithms are reduced to FPP and GP with the *exact* and *minimum* policies. Furthermore, it is possible to use FPP and GP in parallel and to adjust the scheduling parameters dynamically. The mixed FPP/GP scheduling first executes all threads scheduled by GP within an interval of 100 clock cycles. After all GP threads have received the assigned number of execution cycles, the remaining cycles of the interval are used by FPP threads. The *GP minimum* scheduling class is emulated by a combination of GP and FPP scheduling: GP is activated with an exact number of execution cycles and the thread is executed with the required number of cycles during the GP phase. Afterward, the same thread is scheduled using FPP, i.e. it receives additional execution cycles depending on its priority compared to the other FPP threads.

The *jamuth* can also be used in a multicore system [UHR 09a]. Multiple *jamuth* IP cores have to be connected to the identical Avalon busses whereat the data bus can contain a shared cache. The data consistency problem of this configuration is the reason why the *jamuth* does not contain a local data cache. A suitable garbage collection for the multicore systems is also available [UHR 09b].

6.1.5. *Conclusion*

The *Komodo* microcontroller offers a predictable timing behavior and several thread scheduling algorithms that are suitable for hard real-time environments. The GP scheduling allows for a continuous progress of a thread that requires a static data rate. It is also used for the garbage collection, which can now be executed steadily without interruption. From the application's point of view, the garbage collection does not require exclusive execution time, i.e. no stop-the-world behavior is caused by the garbage collection.

The further development of *Komodo*, which is called *jamuth*, allows a very flexible use of the Java processor in so-called System-on-Programmable-Chip (SOPC) designs with Altera FPGAs. This flexibility has to be paid for by a less strict memory interface timing behavior and, hence, a more complex timing model is required for the static WCET analysis. An internal scratchpad compensated this drawback on the instruction path.

In the future, it will be possible to extend the processor core by some separated data caches. Because of the nature of Java bytecodes, it is possible to distinguish between accesses to variables with a static address and those that are allocated dynamically. In addition, a large number of memory accesses are required by the Java environment, which are mostly accesses to read-only values. If multiple caches were implemented, e.g. one cache for each of the three types of memory accesses mentioned, a static analysis could take advantage of the better predictability of the caches' state, resulting in a tighter WCET analysis.

6.2. The JOP architecture

The JOP [SCH 08, SCH 09a] shown in Figure 6.3 is a small processor core for embedded Java systems. Moreover, JOP provides a restricted Java subsystem that is suitable for embedded hard real-time systems.

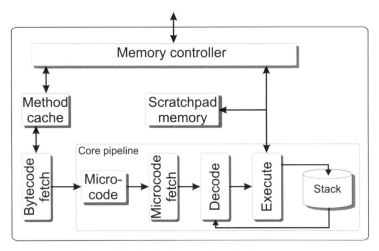

Figure 6.3. *Block diagram of the* JOP *processor*

JOP comprises a three-staged execution pipeline capable of executing microcoded instructions (see *core pipeline* in Figure 6.3). A fourth stage is responsible for bytecode-to-microcode translation, i.e. the instructions executed by JOP are original Java bytecode instructions. These bytecodes are internally translated to sequences of microcodes.

Java bytecode operates on a runtime stack, i.e. is no conventional register file is required. This stack including the stack management is implemented inside the JOP pipeline using a simple dual-ported memory with one read and one write port. Dual read access to the stack is required only for the two upper elements, which are stored in two separate registers that can be accessed directly by the execution stage. The simple implementation of the stack memory allows the implementation of a large stack that is able to hold the runtime variables of multiple nested functions. In addition, administrational information such as the return program counter (PC) is stored on that stack.

Bytecode instructions are fetched out of a special method cache [SCH 04b] exclusively. This cache always holds (at least) the complete actually executed function. In addition, other functions can be available according to the used eviction strategy and the actual execution path. This type of cache guarantees that cache misses can occur only at method boundaries. Since JOP is designed for very small Java systems, a static RAM

(SRAM) as main memory is sufficient and used for instructions and data. Hereby, the method cache prevents conflicts of data and instruction accesses because execution is stalled during the loading of a method.

6.2.1. *Conclusion*

JOP provides advantages regarding predictability compared to other conventional processors. First, the stack cache avoids an additional runtime stack and the save/restore procedures of the register file at function calls and returns. This improves performance and reduces the number of memory accesses significantly, including the number of cache accesses. Second, the method cache prevents conflicts at the memory interface and focuses cache misses (cache analysis) to method boundaries. Third, the minimum size of the executable memory image, caused by the high code density of Java bytecode, allows us to use a small (but expensive) SRAM with simple timing behavior.

6.3. The PRET architecture

The *pre*cision *t*imed (PRET) machine is a multithreaded single-core system. The major target is to provide an exact timing of each processor instruction, independent from dependencies to other instructions. Moreover, the PRET architecture provides special instructions supporting timing. These instructions force the pipeline to stall thread execution until a given deadline or period has passed.

6.3.1. *PRET pipeline architecture*

PRET provides multiple thread slots that are executed round-robin on a cycle-by-cycle basis [EDW 09]. The number of slots must be equal to or greater than the number of pipeline stages. Hence, only a single instruction per thread is available at a time. If a thread slot is empty, pipeline bubbles will be inserted. Using this kind of multithreading, no data forwarding or branch prediction is required because there are sufficient cycles between consecutive instructions of the same thread. Data and control conflicts cannot occur.

To avoid resource conflicts at the memory interface, a memory with multiple memory banks is assumed. Each thread slot can access only one of these banks. Accesses to other banks are not possible. This technique prevents from conflicts when accessing the row buffer of a dynamic memory because each bank is equipped with its own buffer. Row access and precharge can be done individually per bank without harming the row buffers of the other banks and threads, respectively.

6.3.2. Instruction set extension

The PRET idea introduces four instructions that bring time into the low-level instruction execution [BRO 13]. These instructions can be used for checking given deadlines and for artificially extending the execution time of a code snippet to a given extend.

The latter allows us to adjust the actual execution of a function or an application to a given schedule. Hereby, the analyzed timing behavior of a code snippet can be ensured or a desired timing can be enforced.

The proposed PRET extension brings control of timing into the pure functional alignment of standard instruction set architectures (ISAs). Accordingly, the targeted PRET infrastructure will provide a tool-chain that allows for the propagation of the timing behavior expressed on the modeling level down to the actual application execution.

6.3.3. DDR2 memory controller

Since the PRET architecture does not foresee caches, it is not required to read/write larger packets, such as cache lines, from/to the memory. Accordingly, longer burst accesses to the dynamic RAM (DRAM) are not required. Instead, only accesses with the width of a (processor) word are performed resulting in short bursts, if at all.

Even though the basic idea of the PRET memory controller [REI 11] is identical to the ideas of MERASA and T-CREST to sections 6.5 and 6.6, i.e. privatization of banks, a unique feature improves its predictability: DRAM refresh cycles are not scheduled by the memory controller and, hence, are independent from the processor and application. Instead, refresh commands are issued to the banks individually in case the application is not executing a memory access. For example, each branch or jump instruction sends a refresh command to the private bank of the actual thread slot [EDW 09]. This technique prevents unpredictable delays of memory accesses because of refresh commands.

6.3.4. *Conclusion*

The great advantage of the PRET idea is to bring timing down to program execution. This is reached by the four additional instructions targeting timing behavior and by the special pipeline architecture together with the DRAM memory management.

Unfortunately, the round-robin thread scheduling decreases the single-threaded performance to $\frac{1}{n}$ of the overall performance where n is the number of hardware thread slots. Hence, from a single-threaded viewpoint, the performance of PRET is equal to that of a non-pipelined processor. On the other hand, the multithreading allows for a significant performance improvement of parallel applications. This parallelism can be exploited if the parallel threads do not share much data since a thread cannot access the data in the DRAM section (bank) of other threads. Instead, data exchange between threads must be performed through a small and fast scratchpad RAM.

6.4. The multi-issue *CarCore* processor

The *CarCore* processor is based on the architecture of Infineon's TriCore microcontroller core [INF 08], which contains three parallel execution pipelines. One of these execution pipelines is able to execute only a small number of special loop instructions. The other two execution pipelines contain their own register files of 16 registers each. Instructions are statically assigned to one of the two main execution pipelines (except for the mentioned loop instructions).

In contrast to the TriCore, the *CarCore* contains only the two main execution pipelines. The special loop instructions are executed by one of the other pipelines, depending on the registers that are used. The main improvement of the *CarCore* is the multithreading extension including a thread scheduling that exceeds the abilities of the *Komodo* scheduler. A two-layer scheduler enables the *CarCore* to execute more threads in a real-time capable way than thread slots are available. No additional software scheduler is required. The architecture as well as the integrated thread scheduling is described in the following sections.

6.4.1. *The CarCore architecture*

The backend of the CarCore processor (see Figure 6.4) is similar to Infineon's TriCore 1 processor. It features two execution pipelines: one for data arithmetics and one for address calculations and memory accesses. Each one consists of the three stages *decode*, *execute* and *write back*. A detailed description of the differences between the *CarCore* and the TriCore processors is given by Mische *et al.* [MIS 10b].

The preceding two front-end stages, *instruction fetch* and *schedule*, are shared between both execution pipelines and deviate from the TriCore 1 processor. Instructions are issued in order and two instructions from one thread can be issued in parallel, if and only if an address instruction directly follows an integer instruction. Otherwise, the other pipeline is filled by an instruction of another thread. In the case where two instructions of the identical thread are issued, these instructions can also be dependent, i.e. the second instruction requires the result of the first instruction. A special forwarding and execution technique allows us to execute these two instructions in the same clock cycle.

The in-order issue is an important difference to other simultaneous multithreading (SMT) implementations that use out-of-order execution, where lots of resources are shared between the threads (i.e. instruction issue queue, reorder buffer, etc.). In the case of an SMT processor, in-order execution is not necessarily decreasing performance [MOO 04], but simplifies design and reduces hardware costs. Moreover, the architecture of the *CarCore* is free of timing anomalies due to the static assignment of the instructions to the execution units.

Because the TriCore instruction set provides 16 and 32 bit instructions, the fetch stage is designed to fetch two to four instructions of the same thread per cycle by its 64 bit wide memory port. The instructions are buffered in one of the *IWs*, each dedicated to a thread slot.

The scheduling stage implements the first scheduling layer performing a simple priority-based scheduling. It predecodes the instructions depending on the priorities of the thread slots and assigns them to the appropriate pipelines. In the case of latencies, instructions of the next prior thread are selected. The priorities of the thread slots are assigned by an external signal from the *thread manager*, which implements the second scheduling layer. Each priority is within the range of 0 to $\#threadslots - 1$, where 0 is the highest priority.

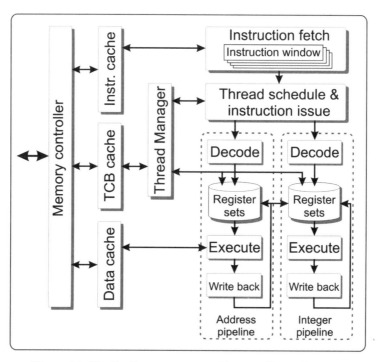

Figure 6.4. *The CarCore processor architecture. The caches are currently not implemented*

6.4.2. *Layered thread scheduling*

The hardware thread scheduling is divided into two layers. The first layer is located deep inside the processor core as the *schedule stage* in the pipeline. It is responsible for a high pipeline utilization.

The second layer is implemented as an independent hardware module besides the processor pipeline, called *thread manager*, to overcome the limited number of hardware thread slots. The *thread manager* is responsible for the management of a list of virtual thread slots. This list contains an arbitrary number of threads including all context information of the threads, i.e. the number of threads is only restricted by the available memory. Each thread is identified by its *thread control block (TCB)*. A TCB is 256 bytes long and contains the thread context as well as scheduling information assigned to this thread.

The *thread manager* autonomously swaps threads from the thread list into the physical hardware thread slots and vice versa. Its actions depend on the (real-time) scheduling parameters of the threads and the progress of the thread execution within the *CarCore* pipelines. Therefore, it receives information about the scheduling from the first layer scheduler within the processor pipeline. On the basis of this information, several (real-time) scheduling algorithms can be implemented within the *thread manager*.

6.4.2.1. *First layer: schedule stage*

As the first layer is integrated as a discrete pipeline stage, it must be small and quick and thus only performs a simple scheduling with fixed priorities. The major task of the first layer is to issue thread slot instructions with the highest priority as fast as possible to the execution pipelines. Emerging latencies (because of memory accesses or branches) are filled with instructions from other active thread slots to keep the utilization of the processor as high as possible.

For a scheduling decision, the first layer requires three facts about each thread slot: if there is a valid instruction within the IW of a thread slot and if so, its priority for scheduling. In addition, it needs information about the previously executed instructions and their latencies. For every pipeline, it picks the instruction of the thread slot with the highest priority and an appropriate instruction, which is not delayed by a branch or a memory access. The decision of which thread slot instructions were assigned to which pipeline is reported to the second layer of the scheduling. This information allows the second layer to count the real execution time of a thread, which is required for some sophisticated scheduling algorithms (see section 6.4.3).

6.4.2.2. *Second layer: thread manager*

The second layer is the more complex of the two-layer scheduling. It analyzes the scheduling information (deadlines, priorities, lists, execution of thread slots, etc.) and reduces it to simple priorities for the first layer. Therefore, it determines the most urgent threads to be scheduled next depending on the appointed scheduling strategy and induces that these threads are assigned to the thread slots of the first layer. If a thread terminates or another thread with a higher priority occurs, the *thread manager* initiates a substitution of one currently executed thread by a thread waiting in the TCB list.

At the beginning of a substitution, the corresponding thread slot is suspended and its context is copied to its TCB in the memory (*Swap Out*). Afterward, the context of the new thread is read from its TCB and written into the hardware thread slot (*Swap In*).

In contrast to common schedulers, this substitution is done by dedicated hardware that works in parallel to the normal program execution and therefore does not block the processor pipeline. It takes 44 cycles on the *CarCore* and the only impact on the processor performance is that the first layer scheduler has to choose instructions from a decreased number of active thread slots.

6.4.3. *CarCore thread scheduling algorithms*

The two-layer *CarCore* thread scheduler provides three different scheduling techniques in parallel. Depending on the criticality of each thread, it can be scheduled by one of the offered techniques. All three techniques are based on so-called *rounds* that are similar to the intervals of the GP scheduling of the *Komodo* scheduler. But, in contrast to the intervals, the length of the rounds can be defined by software and the particular value must be determined by the schedulability analysis. The scheduling techniques are as follows:

– *Dominant time slicing (DTS)*: the DTS scheduling is suitable for hard real-time tasks. At the beginning of each round, all DTS threads are executed for the predefined number of pipeline clock cycles. The sum of the assigned clock cycles must not exceed the length of the rounds. Only a single DTS thread is executed at a time.

– *Periodic instruction quantum (PIQ)*: threads with soft real-time requirements can be scheduled by the PIQ scheduling. Each PIQ thread is executed exactly as many instructions as given by the scheduling parameter.

After the required number of instructions are executed, the thread is substituted by another PIQ thread. PIQ threads are executed in parallel to and after the DTS threads. The difference between DTS and PIQ is that DTS counts the elapsed pipeline cycles whereas PIQ counts the executed instructions.

– *Round robin slicing (RRS)*: the RRS scheduling is used for non-real-time threads. After all DTS and PIQ threads are executed, the threads scheduled by RRS will be swapped in. In contrast to DTS and PIQ, which reset their TCB pointers at the beginning of each round to the start of the corresponding TCB list, the RRS scheduler selects the threads continuously out of its list. Hence, it is not guaranteed that each thread is executed in every round.

Figure 6.5 shows how the three scheduling techniques are unified in a single multithreaded processor core. Two thread slots are required for the DTS scheduling while PIQ and RRS share the remaining slots. If the time required for the DTS threads is shorter than the length of the rounds, the two slots can also be used for PIQ and RRS. The DTS and the PIQ scheduling techniques are described in more detail by Mische *et al*. [MIS 10c] and are summarized in the following sections.

Figure 6.5. *Unified DTS, PIQ and RRS scheduling in one round of length R pipeline clock cycles [MIS 10c]*

6.4.3.1. *Dominant time slicing*

The DTS scheduling is able to execute multiple hard real-time threads on an in-order SMT processor. Especially, it is possible to execute more hard real-time threads than physical thread slots are available. The WCET analysis (required for the schedulability analysis) can be performed for each thread separately and context switching times need not to be taken into account. This is because the context switch is hidden by the switching hardware and the multithreaded execution. The DTS scheduling guarantees that each thread shows the same timing behavior as if it had been executed as single thread with one exception. Because of the dilated execution in multiple rounds, the thread's overall WCET is stretched according to the relationship of the round length and the thread's time slice.

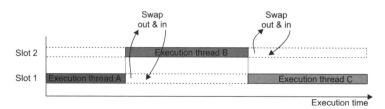

Figure 6.6. *Execution of DTS threads A, B and C in two physical thread slots*

To guarantee the unmodified timing behavior of each hard real-time thread, only one of the DTS threads is executed at a time (see Figure 6.6). In parallel, a further thread is prepared for execution in a second thread slot but this slot is not yet activated. After the first thread has received its time quantum, i.e. it is executed the assigned number of cycles, the first slot is deactivated and the second slot is activated. Now, the second thread is executed according to its time quantum. In parallel, the first thread is swapped out to its TCB and the third thread is swapped into the same physical thread slot. This procedure is repeated until the end of the DTS TCB list is reached. Afterward, the end of the round is awaited and the schedule starts again at the beginning of the list.

Unfortunately, the DTS scheduling blocks two physical thread slots all the time, whereupon only one thread is active. But the advantages still dominate this drawback. The timing of each hard real-time thread is kept constant with respect to its WCET analysis and a special factor that depends on the assigned time slice and the length of the rounds. In addition, the context switching time is completely hidden and, hence, needs not be taken into account at the schedulability analysis. The only precondition is that the time slices of all threads are longer than the time required for swapping out and in the threads in the inactive slot.

The reason why only one thread is executed at a time and the second thread has to wait until the first thread finishes is the timing behavior of the second thread (see Mische *et al.* [MIS 09]). If it were executed in parallel, it would receive several execution cycles in the pipelines that are currently not used by the first thread. But it is not possible to count these execution cycles in terms of pipeline clock cycles that would be required in the case where the thread is the only one. Hence, the parallel execution of the second thread would not bring any advantage because it has to be assumed that the thread starts execution after the quantum of the first thread is fulfilled. Instead, the free execution cycles not used by the active DTS thread are used by the PIQ scheduling described in the next section.

6.4.3.2. *Periodic instruction quantum*

In contrast to DTS, PIQ is able to guarantee a minimum number of executed instructions within a given round (same as used for DTS). The desired number of instructions are given as scheduling parameters in the thread's TCB. Unfortunately, it is not possible to guarantee any arbitrary number of instructions to be executed. Instead, the assigned number of instructions has to be less than or equal to the minimum instruction per cycle (IPC) count that the thread can reach if it runs in single-threaded mode. Therefore, the maximum possible instruction quantum has to be determined in advance by executing the thread in single-threaded mode while measuring the IPC in short periods (less than the length of the rounds). Afterward, the minimum IPC represents[1] the number of instructions that can be guaranteed by the PIQ scheduling to be executed in multithreaded mode.

In contrast to the single-threaded execution, in which the thread is temporarily able to reach a higher IPC, the PIQ scheduler restricts the IPC to nearly the requested one. Hence, a WCET analysis that is done in single-threaded mode is no more valid anymore because the execution is slowed down. But, due to the guaranteed throughput, soft real-time threads can be scheduled using the PIQ scheduling technique.

The implementation of PIQ scheduling is very similar to DTS scheduling. The difference is that the scheduler has to count the executed instruction instead of the elapsed execution cycles. In addition, it is possible to execute multiple PIQ threads in parallel and also in parallel to the active DTS thread. If a thread has reached its cycle quantum, it will be swapped out and another PIQ thread will be swapped into the same physical thread slot. If the end of the PIQ TCB list is reached, the PIQ scheduling is deactivated for the current round and the RRS scheduling is activated to schedule non-real-time threads. A detailed description of the PIQ scheduling including the principles of a schedulability analysis is given by Mische *et al.* [MIS 09].

---

1 By multiplying the IPC with the length of the round.

6.4.4. *Conclusion*

Besides the completely different ISA, the *CarCore* extends the features of the *Komodo* in two directions: first, the *CarCore* is a multi-issue processor with two execution units and, thus, it is able to execute up to two instructions in a single cycle. Second, it is able to schedule and execute a higher number of real-time threads than physical thread slots are available.

The first extension requires the WCET analysis tool to deal with the two execution units, but because of the static assignment no timing anomalies can occur. Hence, the analysis overhead is feasible. In contrast, no additional effort has to be spent on the higher number of supported threads. This is due to the scheduling as well as to the context switch overhead, which is transparent to the threads and needs not to be taken into account at the analysis phase.

Currently, no caches are implemented in the *CarCore* processor. But, with regard to an improved performance of several threads, a cache similar to that of the MERASA processor (see section 6.5.4) could be integrated. Herewith, each of the threads can be assigned to one or more cache banks resulting in a lower memory pressure, higher throughput and still a predictable behavior. The predictability is preserved because each thread holds its own cache portion with its own cache state. Of course, a technique to keep the cache portions coherent must be integrated.

6.5. The MERASA multicore processor

The MERASA multicore processor allows for the parallel execution of multiple threads with hard real-time requirements. In contrast to the multithreaded processor cores described in the previous sections, the MERASA multicore executes hard real-time threads really in parallel and not in an overlapped parallel manner. Static as well as measurement-based WCET analyses are supported (see Rochange *et al.* [ROC 10]). The used processor core is a modified *CarCore*. The number of cores is configurable in the range of 1 core up to 8 cores. The MERASA processor also features a central cache that can be assigned to the cores in different ways and for different functionalities.

The following sections describe the MERASA overall architecture with some details about the interconnection bus and the memory hierarchy. The modifications of the processor core are also presented.

6.5.1. *The MERASA architecture*

Figure 6.7 shows a block diagram of the MERASA architecture. The modified *CarCore* processors are connected by a shared bus system directly to the memory interface and to a central cache that contains multiple cache banks. The cache is also connected to the memory interface. Besides the processor cores, a central *thread manager* is responsible for the initial distribution of the threads to the cores (not shown in the figure).

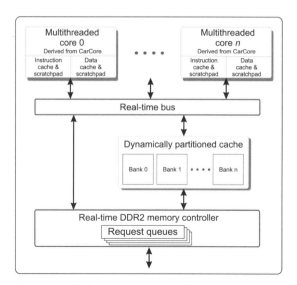

Figure 6.7. *The MERASA system architecture [UNG 10]*

The MERASA processor is designed to execute threads with hard real-time requirements as well as threads with soft or non-real-time requirements. Each core is able to execute up to one hard real-time thread and several soft and non-real-time threads, depending on the number of physical thread slots. The dynamic swapping provided by the *CarCore* is not available in the MERASA processor.

6.5.2. *The MERASA processor core*

The processor core that is integrated in the MERASA multicore processor contains nearly the same pipeline as the *CarCore* processor. But because the MERASA core cannot access the memory directly and because of the different scheduling policies compared to the *CarCore*, several modifications have been applied. The major changes are described in the following:

– *Scheduling*: due to the fixed assignment of hard and non-hard real-time threads to the thread slots, the second scheduling layer is omitted. Instead, the priorities of the thread slots correspond to the slot number where slot 0 has the highest priority. In addition, a thread control interface was added that allows an external unit, the so-called thread manager, to initialize and activate individual thread slots.

– *Instruction fetching*: the memory pressure within a multicore architecture increases with the number of cores. To avoid empty IWs inside the pipeline because of long memory access latencies, the MERASA core was equipped with two local instruction memory systems: a dynamic instruction scratchpad for the hard real-time thread and a standard instruction cache for the other threads.

– *Data accesses*: for the same reason that the fetch path was adapted, the data path was also extended by a local static data scratchpad and a local data cache. The scratchpad is available for the hard real-time thread and should be used for the runtime stack of the thread and other private data. The data cache is available for all other non-hard real-time threads.

– *Bus interface*: the bus interface combines requests from the data as well as from the instruction path. It has to take care of the priorities of the individual requests. In contrast to the *CarCore* where memory requests are immediately processed, the MERASA core has to keep the record of the requests and their sources. This is because an active non-hard real-time request may not have been processed by the interconnection bus while a hard real-time request occurs. In this case, the hard real-time request has to be preferred and the non-hard real-time request must be postponed.

Because the MERASA project especially targets hard real-time threads, only the architectural requirements for this kind of thread are fully implemented in the prototype. The local cache memories for the non-hard real-time threads are foreseen but not yet integrated.

6.5.3. *Interconnection bus*

The interconnect of the multicore system is a bus system. The arbitration mechanism is a hybrid priority and time slice based algorithm. In general, each core has assigned its own time slice for accesses with hard real-time requirements. If one core does not use its time slice for a hard real-time access while a second core requests for such an access, the access of the second core is preferred.

The advantage of this technique is the fast progress of the hard real-time threads. Unfortunately, the soft and non-real-time threads may starve out if too much hard real-time accesses are available. Because of the design of the processor core, which is free of timing anomalies, the variable bus access times do not compromise the static predictability of the architecture.

To enable the real-time bus arbiter to distinguish between hard real-time requests and non-hard real-time requests, each bus master has to deliver the type of the access. Hence, the processor cores must be aware of the real-time class of the executed threads.

6.5.4. *Memory hierarchy*

A highlight of the MERASA architecture is the configurable memory hierarchy. The central cache is organized in multiple cache banks and each of them can be assigned to a different core. In addition, the functionality of the cache banks is not fixed: each one can be used in one of the following ways.

– *First-level data cache*: because of consistency problems, the hard real-time threads do not use the local cache inside each core. Instead, a configurable number of cache banks can be used as first-level data caches. In addition, it is possible to define a cache bank as private to a thread or as possibly shared, i.e. the bank may be reconfigured to belong to another core. This feature allows multiple hard real-time threads to communicate and cooperate on shared data.

– *Second-level data cache*: non-hard real-time threads are allowed to use the local data cache inside each core as first-level data cache. Hence, the central cache may serve as a second-level cache. It may or may not be shared between multiple cores. Of course, a consistency technique must be implemented in this case but non-hard real-time threads are beyond the scope of the MERASA project that especially targets hard real-time applications.

– *Instruction cache*: a cache bank can also serve as an instruction cache for both hard and non-hard real-time threads. In the case of a hard real-time thread, the cache acts as a second level after the local scratchpad, i.e. it reduces the pressure on the memory interface. For non-hard real-time threads, it forms a standard second-level cache behind the local instruction cache.

A bypass connection besides the central cache is also available. This bypass allows direct accesses to the memory that is needed for non-cached accesses. These accesses are required for direct communication between different threads, in particular, lock variables that need atomic read-modify-write accesses use this link.

The memory controller itself is also designed in an analyzable way. It is based on burst accesses that form a complete cache line (see Paolieri *et al.* [PAO 09b]). The arbitration technique is similar to that of the real-time interconnection bus. This means that the real-time class of a request is also required by the memory controller. A special feature is a third type of memory operation (besides *read* and *write*): the *read–write* operation. The *read–write* operation allows to perform an atomic read-and-write operation on the same address. This operation only targets a smaller data width (32 bit) but it fits completely into the time frame of a standard cache line access.

The *read–write* operation allows to handle lock variables in an atomic way without the need for bus/memory locks. Hence, it is not required that the static WCET analysis takes into account possible bus/memory locks from other cores.

6.5.5. *Conclusion*

The MERASA architecture offers a flexible solution for systems with hard real-time requirements as well as for mixed critical systems. A memory hierarchy that provides local and also global caches and scratchpads allows a high computational throughput combined with a tight static analyzability. The central cache can serve as a second-level cache for non-hard real-time threads and as a private first-level cache for hard real-time threads. An appropriate configuration can be assigned for each cache bank separately. An additional feature of the MERASA system is the comfortable memory controller that allows atomic read–write operations without disturbing the analyzable time slice based accesses of other cores.

Further developments of the MERASA architecture could focus on the support of non-hard real-time threads, which is not fully implemented in the current prototype. In addition, cooperating parallel threads that are designed as producer/consumer pairs are very well supported by the current architecture, if only one producer and one consumer are present. In the case of multiple producers/consumer, an enhancement of the central cache has to be developed.

6.6. The T-CREST multicore processor

The T-CREST project targets the real-time constraints of future safety-critical multicore and many-core systems. Therefore, a strictly time-predictable multicore system has been developed, including a suitable processor core, techniques for strictly timed communication structures and a memory controller. The interconnect allows the cores to be treated as independent systems from the timing point of view. Nevertheless, the cores can communicate with each other and with external memories using a time-predictable memory controller.

6.6.1. *The Patmos processor core*

The processor core applied in the T-CREST project is the dual-issue *Patmos* processor [SCH 11]. It is a pipelined core and in principle its ISA follows the reduced instruction set computer (RISC) approach. Moreover, the ISA is fully predicated and up to two instructions can be statically bundled to be executed in parallel. Instructions are fetched out of a local method cache. So, no cache misses can occur in the scope of functions and the core is able to execute one or two instructions per cycle. The only exceptions are branches and memory accesses that can lead to pipeline stalls. The number of conditional branches it minimized by the support of predication and a split-phase load technique is used for memory loads. Hereby, the result of the memory read access is stored in a dedicated register that can be read by a special instruction. In contrast to the CarCore processor, the second part of the load is formed by a separate instruction that must be executed explicitly. Using this technique, the memory access latencies can be at least partly bridged by the execution of independent instructions.

The memory subsystem of Patmos is formed by several caches. As already mentioned, instructions are fetched only from the method cache. This cache is working on the granularity of functions, which means that cache misses can occur only on function boundaries. In addition to the method cache, a stack cache, a constant cache and a data cache are present. The applications runtime stack is cached in a special stack cache [ABB 13], while constant values and data of the working set is cached in associative caches. Hereby, constant data and the working set are handled by different caches with different associativity. It is encoded inside the memory access instructions which cache is used for the corresponding access. In addition to the caches, a local scratchpad memory is also provided to store often used data.

Compared to traditional RISC cores, software development for Patmos looks more complex at first glance. Two instructions are required for memory reads, cache selection for memory accesses and instructions bundling for performance increase. But all these issues can be performed automatically by a compiler and have no (negative) effect to the software developer. Instead, greater effort is spent in programming results in a better timing predictability. There are no instructions with variable timing except for cache accesses that can lead to a hit or a miss (including the method cache). Here, the various caches improve the analyzability of cache behavior resulting in a lower pessimism of a static WCET analysis.

6.6.2. *The T-CREST interconnect*

The T-CREST project is not based on a particular network-on-chip (NoC) architecture. Instead, a static scheduling technique is proposed that offers time-predictable communication. Hereby, an all-to-all communication without any interferences and unpredictable stalling is also possible.

The basic idea of the proposed technique is a network with routing nodes without dynamic routing capabilities. Instead, each router comprises a scheduling table that indicates incoming–outgoing relationships. All routers of the complete interconnect step synchronously through their individual tables (of equal length), which lead to connective (pipelined) paths from source nodes to destination nodes. Each foreseen path is available periodically, depending on the length of the routing tables. There are no buffers available in the routers because transmitted data do not need to be buffered at any time. The absence of buffers reduces the hardware complexity significantly, since not only the buffer memory but also the buffer management is avoided.

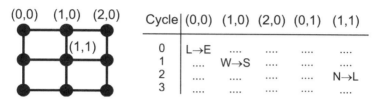

Cycle	(0,0)	(1,0)	(2,0)	(0,1)	(1,1)
0	L→E	....	....	....	....
1	....	W→S	....	....	....
2	....	....	....	....	N→L
3	....	....	....	....	....

Figure 6.8. *Example communication from node (0,0) to (1,1) in a 3 × 3 T-CREST mesh*

Figure 6.8 shows an example of a 3 × 3 mesh interconnect. The given routing tables allow a data transfer from node (0,0) to node (1,1) in three transfer cycles. Each entry specifies the input–output port (N, E, S, W, L) connection in a particular cycle. Besides the single connection per clock cycle and router presented here, other connections (concerning other ports) can also be established in the same router in the same cycle. Moreover, all other routers and empty table entries can establish different data transfers in parallel. Schoeberl *et al.* [SCH 12] have shown that all-to-all communication in a 4 × 4 mesh is possible with a period of only 18 cycles. Of course, if a particular communication matrix is given, this corresponding period is much shorter.

6.6.3. *Conclusion*

T-CREST provides a many-core architecture suitable for hard real-time systems. A central element is the NoC architecture, especially the static routing of data. The proposed routing reduces the hardware complexity of the used routers compared to buffer-based systems with dynamic routing. Moreover, the static approach provides a tightly analyzable timing behavior.

The architecture of the Patmos processor core provides an increased performance compared to a single-issue pipeline by the possible parallel execution of two instructions. This technique is similar to the very long instruction word (VLIW) technique and also applied by Infineon's TriCore processor and the CarCore (see section 6.4), accordingly. As extension to the two other mentioned architectures, Patmos supports multiple data caches that cover different domains of data, namely the runtime stack, static variables and constants, and the working set. Applying multiple caches reduces cross talk of accesses to different data domains and improves predictability of the caches' state.

6.7. The parMERASA manycore processor

The aim of the parMERASA project was to provide a platform suitable for the execution of multiple parallelized real-time applications. Therefore, the system must target two major issues: separation of the different applications as well as tight coupling of the execution units involved in the execution of the parallel parts.

To determine the way of communication, synchronization and coordination between parallel threads, embedded applications from three different application domains have been analyzed. This analysis showed that data as well as control parallelism can be exploited. Synchronization is mainly based on mutexes and barriers. Communication and coordination is based on exchanged messages as well as global variables and data structures.

6.7.1. *System overview*

The focus of parMERASA's hardware architecture is on the memory hierarchy, the interconnection network and an inter-core signaling and communication technique. Hence, the focus is not on the core architecture itself since every application domain has preferences on a particular core. Nevertheless, only one core architecture is used in the parMERASA project acting as a representative for any other suitable architecture.

Since multiple parallel applications executed in parallel need to be supported, a sufficient number of cores is required. Bus-based systems do not scale very well and, hence, a NoC is used as the communication infrastructure. Also the interrupt system and the peripheral devices are connected to this NoC.

6.7.2. *Memory hierarchy*

Since the use of a NoC implies long latencies for accessing remote shared memories, a powerful memory hierarchy is required. Of course, this hierarchy must provide an analyzable timing behavior in addition to efficient memory accesses. To reach that goal, multiple memories are available in the system, local memories and remote memories. Frequently used data such as the runtime stack and private data are stored in local memories while larger portions of shared as well as private data are stored in remote memories. Moreover, the local memories of other cores can also be accessed by any core that is used for message passing. A memory mapping technique allows access to its own local memories at the same address for all cores while accesses to the other local memories are performed using different addresses, depending on the node that has to be accessed. Figure 6.9 shows the used memory map.

While accesses to the local memories are performed by simple accesses to the local interconnect (e.g. a bus connecting the core and the local memories), accesses to remote memories such as the local memories of other cores as well as external memories are translated into NoC messages. These messages are passed through the NoC to the corresponding destination. If necessary, an answer with the requested data is sent back to the initiator.

Obviously, this kind of access to remote data induces a high latency on memory accesses. To efficiently deal with these latencies, local caches are implemented. Hereby, only the data path is taken into account,   for instructions a perfect scratchpad memory is assumed. In practice, a dynamic scratchpad as described by Metzlaff and Ungerer [MET 12] can be used for instruction fetch support.

Since the parMERASA architecture needs to support parallel applications with significant amounts of shared data, the memory hierarchy must provide coherent accesses to this data. This can be done by uncached accesses to the shared memory or by providing a coherency technique of local data caches. Since uncached accesses result in unacceptably long latencies, a suitable coherence technique is required. The *on-demand coherence cache* (ODC^2, see section 5.4.2) has been developed within the parMERASA project. It provides coherent accesses to shared data together with the advantages of caching. Moreover, ODC^2 provides analyzable timing behavior together with the previously requested properties:

– Coherent accesses to shared data: there are no data present in more than one local cache at any time. Coherency is preserved by mutual exclusion and the automatic write back and reload of ODC^2.

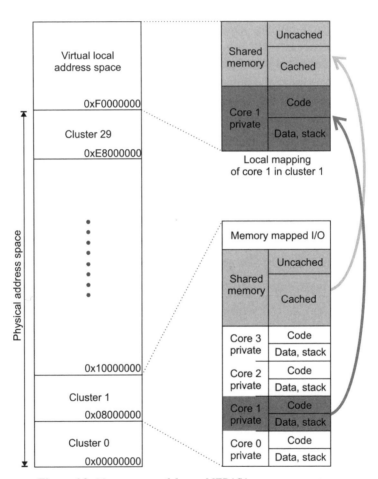

Figure 6.9. *Memory map of the parMERASA many-core system with a maximum of 30 clusters and four cores per cluster. Local code and data as well as shared data sections are accessible at identical addresses for all cores in all clusters*

– Isolation of cores: since there are no coherence messages exchanged between the cores, all cores act independently.

– Advantage of caching: ODC^2 is taking advantage of temporal and spatial locality of accesses to private data as well as to shared data within regions of mutual exclusion.

6.7.3. Communication infrastructure

The high number of requested cores requires an efficient way of communication. Hereby, communication must be possible from any active system (i.e. master) component to any other component. This means that the following communication links must be possible:

– *Core to node communication*: hereby, any core should be able to communicate with any other network node. This is required to access remote local memories for passing messages from one node to an other node.

– *Core to external memory*: each node (i.e. each core within a node) requires access to external memories in order to read/write large amounts of private as well as shared data.

– *Core to input/output (I/O)*: cores must be able to communicate with peripheral devices. This is required for initialization as well as for exchange of I/O data.

– *I/O to memory (local and external)*: larger amounts of I/O data need to be transferred by direct memory access (DMA) operations. Therefore, the I/O system, including the DMA controller, must be able to communicate with external memories and also with local memories.

In general, a simple bus-based architecture using time division multiple access (TDMA) arbitration would provide all these features, including the previously mentioned isolation of applications. Unfortunately, busses do not scale very well and so this kind of architecture is not suitable for the targeted number of cores.

As a result, parMERASA will investigate two different kinds of NoCs (see Figure 6.10): a clustered bus system and a mesh supporting virtual channels. The virtual channels will be used to form virtual clusters among the nodes.

Clustering is required to provide isolation between different applications running in parallel on the parMERASA architecture.

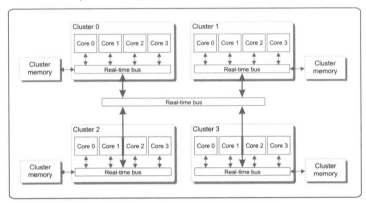

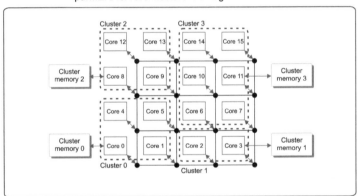

Figure 6.10. *Investigated parMERASA topologies*

The clustered bus architecture supports clusters by default. Unfortunately, it is extremely unflexible since the clusters are fixed. But, together with a TDMA-based bus arbitration, it is also possible to allow flexibility to a limited extend. This limitation is based on the bus structure and the number of sections that must be passed if parts of an application are located in different hardware clusters.

The mesh-based systems allow us to place the different parts of an application close to each other. Hence, the communication does not need to be shared with other applications, except for some special locations at the border of an application area and the transit traffic. These situations will be addressed by virtual channels that use a hardware arbitration such as TDMA.

Independent from the selected NoC architecture, parMERASA distinguishes between intra-cluster and inter-cluster communications. Intra-cluster communication has priority over inter-cluster communication since it is assumed that the former occurs much more frequently than the latter. Moreover, intra-cluster communication also carries memory accesses to and from the cluster's memory that means that delaying these messages would harm the performance. Inter-core communication is less frequent and a longer latency can be accepted in this case.

6.7.4. *Peripheral devices and interrupt system*

The parMERASA architecture targets real-world applications that are parallelized for increased performance. For these application types, input data from peripheral devices are required and output data are generated. Therefore, the parMERASA architecture is equipped with a flexible I/O system including a signaling technique.

6.7.4.1. *I/O devices*

The integrated peripheral devices include a virtual controller area network (CAN) interface and a generic I/O module, which can emulate digital I/O, pulse width modulation (PWM) generation as well as analog-to-digital and digital-to-analog converters. For both devices, the input data are provided by a trace file that specifies time-stamped input data. As output, another file is generated representing the output generated by the simulated application. Hence, the system can be evaluated by comparing the output trace files. Hereby, the design space can be evaluated with respect to different ways of parallelization as well as different topologies.

All I/O devices are implemented as memory-mapped I/O and comprise a small internal memory as well as control registers that can be accessed through the NoC. Additional DMA functionality is currently not integrated, instead the data have to be placed into the internal memory or read from there, respectively.

6.7.4.2. *Signaling infrastructure*

The signaling technique is based on two types of components: *Smart Interrupt Controller (SIC)* and *Tiny Interrupt Controller (TIC)*. One TIC is available in every cluster containing processor cores, i.e. all clusters contain one TIC. In contrast, SICs are available only in clusters with peripheral components with interrupt capabilities. Precisely, a SIC is connected to interrupt sources while TICs establish connections to interrupt destinations. The communication between SICs and TICs is performed by the NoC and, hence, relies on the real-time capabilities of the NoC.

Each SIC comprises a pair of internal control registers per interrupt channel, i.e. per supported interrupt source. These registers specify the destination (TIC) of the interrupt together with a magic number. In case of an interrupt, the magic number is sent to the TIC that activates the interrupt request of the corresponding target core. The core can identify the interrupt source by reading the magic number from the TIC. Because of the required configuration of the SICs' control registers, the signaling system is extremely flexible.

Moreover, the TICs can also be accessed by conventional write accesses of the cores. Hence, an inter-core signaling can also be implemented by this technique. Therefore, a core needs to write a magic number (different from the numbers used by the I/O devices) to a TIC's internal register. The destination core can identify the signaling by the magic number.

To improve the latency at any signaling action, the dedicated magic numbers are not chosen artificially. Instead, the magic numbers are exactly the pointer to the handling routine of the particular event. This technique significantly simplifies the assignment of the signaling source and handling routine, since it is not required to enquire a mapping table. The received magic number is directly used as the argument of an indirect jump.

Unfortunately, the proposed SIC/TIC infrastructure cannot be used for multi- and broadcasts. Therefore, a *multicast interrupt controller* (MIC) is used. A MIC combines parts of the functionalities of a TIC and a SIC with additional multicast features. In contrast to SIC and TIC, MIC does not provide any direct link to interrupt sources or destinations. A MIC is connected only to the NoC (possibly within a cluster). The task of a MIC is triggered by a write access to its trigger register. Following this write access, an internal list of accesses is executed. Each entry in this list is a triple of a target address, a magic number and a waiting time. The first two define target TIC and corresponding magic number while the last one defines the waiting period before the next access is triggered.

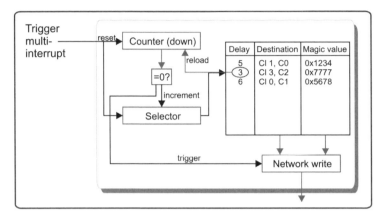

Figure 6.11. *Block diagram of the parMERASA multicast interrupt controller (MIC)*

Figure 6.11 shows a block diagram of a MIC. The principal idea of the MIC is to send a multicast signal to several cores in parallel. Moreover, the signal should reach the destinations (more or less) simultaneously. Therefore, the waiting periods need to be defined according to the different times required by the messages to reach their destination. The message with the highest distance to its destination has to be placed first in the list while the nearest target must be the last entry. The actual time at which the messages reach their destination depends on the time predictability of the NoC. Possibly, a certain jitter must be accepted. For example, if the T-CREST NoC technology is applied, this jitter will most probably appear since it is not possible for a core to receive messages in any arbitrary cycle. Moreover, it is also not possible to send the messages with the given waiting periods because the time at which a message can be sent depends on the destination (see section 6.6.2).

6.7.5. *Conclusion*

The parMERASA architecture shows conceptual directions toward a time-predictable many-core architecture. Starting from simple processor cores, techniques for a time analyzable interconnection structure are presented. This technique distinguishes between inter-cluster and intra-cluster communications and allows freedom from interference for inter-cluster communication. Efficient memory accesses, also for shared data, are enabled by the ODC^2, which allows for a more flexible data and memory layout than the proposed MERASA cache structure. Interaction between the environment and the cores and also between the cores themselves is established by the flexible interrupt and signaling system. Its predictability is based on intra-cluster communication.

Bibliography

[138 96] 13818-2 I., Information technology - generic coding of moving pictures and associated audio information: video, 1996.

[ABB 13] ABBASPOUR S., BRANDNER F., SCHOEBERL M., "A time-predictable stack cache", *Proceedings of the 9th Workshop on Software Technologies for Embedded and Ubiquitous Systems*, Paderborn, Germany, 2013.

[AGA 88] AGARWAL A., SIMONI R., HENNESSY J., *et al.*, "An evaluation of directory schemes for cache coherence", *Proceedings of the 15th Annual International Symposium on Computer architecture, ISCA '88*, IEEE Computer Society Press, Los Alamitos, CA, Honolulu, Hawai, pp. 280–298, 1988.

[AHO 07] AHO A.V., LAM M.S., SETHI R., *et al.*, *Compilers: Principles, Techniques, & Tools*, vol. 1009, Pearson/Addison Wesley, 2007.

[AJI 00] AJILE, aJ-100 Real-time Low Power Java Processor, Preliminary data sheet, 2000.

[ALT 96a] ALT M., FERDINAND C., MARTIN F., *et al.*, "Cache behavior prediction by abstract interpretation", *Static Analysis Symposium (SAS)*, Springer, Aachen, Germany, 1996.

[ALT 96b] ALTENBERND P., "On the false path problem in hard real-time programs", *Euromicro Workshop on Real-Time Systems*, IEEE, pp. 102–107, L'Aquila, Italy, 1996.

[ALT 12] ALTMEYER S., DAVIS R.I., MAIZA C., "Improved cache related pre-emption delay aware response time analysis for fixed priority pre-emptive systems", *Real-Time Systems*, vol. 48, no. 5, pp. 52–66, 2012.

[ASA 07] ASADUZZAMAN A., LIMBACHIYA N., MAHGOUB I., *et al.*, "Evaluation of I-cache locking technique for real-time embedded systems", *4th International Conference on Innovations in Information Technology, 2007, (IIT '07)*, Dubai, pp. 342–346, November 2007.

[ASA 13] ASAVOAE M., MAIZA C., RAYMOND P., *et al.*, "Program semantics in model-based WCET analysis: a state of the art perspective", *International Workshop on WCET Analysis*, Paris, France, 2013.

[BAL 08] BALLABRIGA C., CASSÉ H., "Improving the first-miss computation in set-associative instruction caches", *Euromicro Conference on Real-Time Systems (ECRTS)*, Prague, Czech Republic, 2008.

[BAL 09] BALLABRIGA C., CASSÉ H., DE MICHIEL M., "A generic framework for blackbox components in WCET computation (regular paper)", *Workshop on Worst-Case Execution Time Analysis*, Dublin, Ireland, 2009.

[BAL 11] BALLABRIGA C., CASSÉ H., ROCHANGE C., *et al.*, "OTAWA: an open toolbox for adaptive wcet analysis", *Proceedings of the Software Technologies for Embedded and Ubiquitous Systems*, Springer, Waidhofen/Ybbs, Austria, pp. 35–46, 2011.

[BAL 12] BALDOVIN A., MEZZETTI E., VARDANEGA T., "A time-composable operating system", *International Workshop on WCET Analysis*, Pisa, Italy, 2012.

[BAR 08] BARRE J., ROCHANGE C., SAINRAT P., "An architecture for the simultaneous execution of hard real-time threads", *International Conference on Embedded Computer Systems: Architectures, Modeling, and Simulation, 2008 (SAMOS 2008)*, IEEE, Samos, Greece, pp. 18–24, 2008.

[BAT 05] BATE I., REUTEMANN R., "Efficient integration of bimodal branch prediction and pipeline analysis", *International Conference on Real-Time Computing Systems and Applications (RCTSA)*, Hong Kong, China, 2005.

[BER 02] BERNAT G., COLIN A., PETTERS S.M., "WCET analysis of probabilistic hard real-time systems", *Real-Time Systems Symposium (RTSS)*, IEEE, pp. 279–288, Austin, USA, 2002.

[BER 06] BERG C., "PLRU cache domino effects", *International Workshop on WCET Analysis*, Dresden, Germany, 2006.

[BET 10] BETTS A., Hybrid measurement-based WCET analysis using instrumentation point graphs, PhD Thesis, University of York, 2010.

[BOD 05] BODIN F., PUAUT I., "A WCET-oriented static branch prediction scheme for real time systems", *Proceedings of the 17th Euromicro Conference on Real-Time Systems (ECRTS '05)*, IEEE Computer Society, Washington, DC, Palma de Mallorca, Spain, pp. 33–40, 2005.

[BOU 10] BOURGADE R., ROCHANGE C., DE MICHIEL M., *et al.*, "MBBA: a multi-bandwidth bus arbiter for hard real-time", *5th International Conference on Embedded and Multimedia Computing (EMC)*, Cebu, Philippines, 2010.

[BRI 02] BRINKSCHULTE U., UNGERER T., *Mikrocontroller und Mikroprozessoren*, Springer-Verlag, Heidelberg, September 2002.

[BRO 13] BROMAN D., ZIMMER M., KIM Y., *et al.*, "Precision timed infrastructure: design challenges", *The Electronic System Level Synthesis Conference (ESLsyn 2013)*, San Francisco, USA, 2013.

[BUR 97] BURGER D., AUSTIN T.M., "The SimpleScalar tool set, version 2.0", *SIGARCH Computer Architecture News*, vol. 25, no. 3, pp. 13–25, 1997.

[BUR 99] BURCHARD L., ALTENBERND P., "Worst-case execution times analysis of MPEG-decoding", *10th Euromicro Workshop on Real Time Systems (WRTS)*, York, UK, 1999.

[BUR 00] BURNS F., KOELMANS A., YAKOVLEV A., "WCET analysis of superscalar processors using simulation with coloured petri nets", *Real-Time Systems*, vol. 18, nos. 2/3, pp. 275–288, 2000.

[BUR 05a] BURGUIERE C., ROCHANGE C., "A contribution to branch prediction modeling in WCET analysis", *Proceedings of the Conference on Design, Automation and Test in Europe (DATE '05)*, IEEE Computer Society, Munich, Germany, Washington DC, pp. 612–617, 2005.

[BUR 05b] BURGUIÈRE C., ROCHANGE C., SAINRAT P., "A case for static branch prediction in real-time systems", *International Conference on Real-Time Computing Systems and Applications (RCTSA)*, Hong Kong, China, 2005.

[BUR 07] BURGUIERE C., ROCHANGE C., "On the complexity of modelling dynamic branch predictors when computing worst-case execution times", *ERCIM/DECOS Workshop on Dependable Embedded Systems*, Nuremberg, Germany, 2007.

[BUS 96] BUSQUETS-MATAIX J.V., SERRANO J.J., ORS R., *et al.*, "Adding instruction cache effect to schedulability analysis of preemptive real-time systems", *Real-Time and Embedded Technology and Applications Symposium (RTAS)*, Boston, USA, 1996.

[CAM 05] CAMPOY A.M., PUAUT I., IVARS A.P., *et al.*, "Cache contents selection for statically-locked instruction caches: an algorithm comparison", *17th Euromicro Conference on Real-Time Systems (ECRTS)*, IEEE, pp. 49–56, Palma de Mallorca, Spain, 2005.

[CAR 04] CARPENTER J., FUNK S., HOLMAN P., *et al.*, "A categorization of real-time multiprocessor scheduling problems and algorithms", *Handbook of Scheduling: Algorithms, Models, and Performance Analysis*, Chapman & Hall, CRC Computer, 2004.

[CAS 13] CASSÉ H., BIRÉE F., SAINRAT P., "Multi-architecture value analysis for machine code", *International Workshop on WCET Analysis*, Paris, France, 2013.

[CAZ 04] CAZORLA F.J., RAMIREZ A., VALERO M., *et al.*, "QoS for high-performance SMT processors in embedded systems", *IEEE Micro*, vol. 24, no. 4, pp. 24–31, 2004.

[CAZ 13] CAZORLA F.J., QUINONES E., VARDANEGA T., *et al.*, "PROARTIS: probabilistically analyzable real-time systems", *ACM Transactions on Embedded Computing Systems (TECS)*, vol. 12, no. 2s, pp. 94:1–94:26, 2013.

[CHE 92] CHEONG H., "Life span strategy – a compiler-based approach to cache coherence", *Proceedings of the 6th International Conference on Supercomputing, (ICS '92)*, ACM, New York, NY, pp. 139–148, Washington, USA, 1992.

[CHO 07] CHO H., EGGER B., LEE J., *et al.*, "Dynamic data scratchpad memory management for a memory subsystem with an MMU", *SIGPLAN Notices*, vol. 42, no. 7, pp. 195–206, 2007.

[CLA 86] CLARKE E.M., EMERSON E.A., *et al.*, "Automatic verification of finite-state concurrent systems using temporal logic specifications", *ACM Transactions on Programming Languages and Systems*, vol. 8, no. 2, pp. 244–263, 1986.

[CME 91] CMELIK R.F., KONG S.I., DITZEL D.R., *et al.*, "An analysis of MIPS and SPARC instruction set utilization on the SPEC benchmarks", *Proceedings of the 4th International Conference on Architectural Support for Programming Languages and Operating Systems*, ACM, New York, NY, pp. 290–302, Santa Clara, USA, 1991.

[COF 76] COFFMAN E., "Introduction to deterministic scheduling theory", *Computer and Job-Shop Scheduling Theory*, John Wiley & Sons, New York, pp. 1–50, 1976.

[COL 00] COLIN A., PUAUT I., "Worst case execution time analysis for a processor with branch prediction", *Real-Time System*, vol. 18, nos. 2/3, pp. 249–274, 2000.

[COO 02] COOPER T.H., WATERMAN T., Building a control-flow graph from scheduled assembly code, Report, Rice University, Texas, USA, 2002.

[COU 77] COUSOT P., COUSOT R., "Abstract interpretation: a unified lattice model for static analysis of programs by construction or approximation of fixpoints", *Proceedings of the 4th ACM SIGACT-SIGPLAN Symposium on Principles of Programming Languages*, ACM, Los Angeles, USA, pp. 238–252, 1977.

[CRO 03] CROWLEY P., BAER J.-L., "Worst-case execution time estimation for hardware-assisted multithreaded processors", *HPCA-9 Workshop on Network Processors*, Anaheim, USA, 2003.

[CUE 11] CUESTA B.A., ROS A., GÓMEZ M.E., *et al.*, "Increasing the effectiveness of directory caches by deactivating coherence for private memory blocks", *Proceedings of the 38th Annual International Symposium on Computer Architecture, (ISCA '11)*, ACM, New York, NY, pp. 93–104, Sanfose, USA, 2011.

[CUL 07] CULLMANN C., MARTIN F., "Data-flow based detection of loop bounds", *7th International Workshop on Worst-Case Execution Time Analysis*, Prague, Czech Republic, 2007.

[CUL 13] CULLMANN C., "Cache persistence analysis: theory and practice", *ACM Transactions on Embedded Computing Systems (TECS)*, vol. 12, no. 1, pp. 40:1–40:25, 2013.

[DAL 10] DALSGAARD A.E., CHR M., TOFT M., *et al.*, "METAMOC: modular execution time analysis using model checking", *WCET, International Workshop on WCET Analysis*, Brussels, Belgium, pp. 113–123, 2010.

[DAR 93] DARNELL E., KENNEDY K., "Cache coherence using local knowledge", *Proceedings of the 1993 ACM/IEEE Conference on Supercomputing, (Supercomputing '93)*, ACM, New York, NY, pp. 720–729, Portland, USA, 1993.

[DAV 11] DAVIS R.I., BURNS A., "A survey of hard real-time scheduling for multiprocessor systems", *ACM Computing Surveys (CSUR)*, vol. 43, no. 4, pp. 35:1–35:44, 2011.

[DE 08] DE MICHIEL M., BONENFANT A., CASSÉ H., *et al.*, "Static loop bound analysis of C programs based on flow analysis and abstract interpretation", *14th IEEE International Conference on Embedded and Real-Time Computing Systems and Applications, (RTCSA '08)*, IEEE, Kaohsiung, Taiwan, pp. 161–166, 2008.

[DE 10] DE MICHIEL M., BONENFANT A., BALLABRIGA C., *et al.*, "Partial Flow Analysis with oRange (short paper)", *ISoLA Symposium On Leveraging Applications of Formal Methods, Verification and Validation*, no. 6416LNCS, Springer, Heraklion, Greece, 2010.

[DER 74] DERTOUZOS M., "Control robotics: the procedural control of physical processes", *Information Processing*, vol. 74, pp. 807–813, 1974.

[DER 89] DERTOUZOS M.L., MOK A.K., "Multiprocessor online scheduling of hard-real-time tasks", *IEEE Transactions on Software Engineering*, vol. 15, no. 12, pp. 1497–1506, 1989.

[DEV 07] DEVERGE J.-F., PUAUT I., "WCET-directed dynamic scratchpad memory allocation of data", *19th Euromicro Conference on Real-Time Systems (ECRTS)*, IEEE, Prague, Czech Republic, 2007.

[DUD 11] DUDZIAK T., HERTER J., "Cache analysis in presence of pointer-based data structures", *SIGBED Review*, vol. 8, no. 3, pp. 7–10, 2011.

[EDW 09] EDWARDS S.A., KIM S., LEE E.A., *et al.*, "A disruptive computer design idea: architectures with repeatable timing", *Proceedings of the IEEE International Conference on Computer Design (ICCD)*, IEEE, Lake Tahoe, CA, October 2009.

[EGG 06] EGGER B., KIM C., JANG C., *et al.*, "A dynamic code placement technique for scratchpad memory using postpass optimization ", *Conference on Compilers, Architecture, and Synthesis for Embedded Systems*, Seoul, Korea, 2006.

[EIS 06] EISINGER J., POLIAN I., BECKER B., *et al.*, "Automatic identification of timing anomalies for cycle-accurate worst-case execution time analysis", *Design and Diagnostics of Electronic Circuits and Systems, 2006 IEEE*, IEEE, Prague, Czech Republic, pp. 13–18, 2006.

[ENG 99] ENGBLOM J., ERMEDAHL A., "Pipeline timing analysis using a trace-driven simulator", *International Conference on Real-Time Computing Systems and Applications (RCTSA)*, Hong Kong, China, 1999.

[ENG 02] ENGBLOM J., Processor pipelines and static worst-case execution time analysis, PhD Thesis, Uppsala University, 2002.

[ERM 07] ERMEDAHL A., SANDBERG C., *et al.*, "Loop bound analysis based on a combination of program slicing, abstract interpretation, and invariant analysis", *7th International Workshop on Worst-Case Execution Time Analysis*, Prague, Czech Republic, 2007.

[ESK 99] ESKICIOGLU M., MARSLAND T., HU W., *et al.*, "Evaluation of the JIAJIA software DSM system on high performance computer architectures", *Proceedings of the 32nd Annual Hawaii International Conference on Systems Sciences, 1999 (HICSS-32)*, vol. Track8, Hawai, USA, p. 10, 1999.

[FAL 07] FALK H., PLAZAR S., THEILING H., "Compile-time decided instruction cache locking using worst-case execution paths", *5th IEEE/ACM International Conference on Hardware/Software Codesign and System Synthesis (CODES+ISSS)*, ACM, Salzburg, Austria, 2007.

[FER 98] FERDINAND C., WILHELM R., "On predicting data cache behavior for real-time systems", *International Conference on Languages, Compilers, and Tools for Embedded Systems (LCTES)*, Montreal, Canada, 1998.

[FER 99a] FERDINAND C., MARTIN F., WILHELM R., *et al.*, "Cache behavior prediction by abstract interpretation", *Science of Computer Programming*, vol. 35, no. 2, pp. 163–189 1999.

[FER 99b] FERDINAND C., WILHELM R., "Efficient and precise cache behavior prediction for real-time systems", *Real-Time Systems*, vol. 17, nos. 2–3, pp. 131–181, 1999.

[FIE 01] FIELDS B., RUBIN S., BODÍK R., "Focusing processor policies via critical-path prediction", *International Symposium on Computer Architecture (ISCA)*, Göthenburg, Sweden, 2001.

[FRE 07] FREDRIKSSON J., NOLTE T., ERMEDAHL A., *et al.*, "Clustering worst-case execution times for software components", *International Workshop on WCET Analysis*, Prague, Czech Republic, 2007.

[FRE 06] FREESCALE SEMICONDUCTOR, "Application Note 2129: Instruction and Data Cache Locking on the e300 Processor Core", July 2006. Available at http://cache.freescale.com/files/netcomm/doc/app_note/AN2129.pdf?fsrch=1&sr=1.

[FUH 01] FUHRMANN S., PFEFFER M., KREUZINGER J., *et al.*, "Real-time garbage collection for a multithreaded Java microcontroller", *International Symposium on Object-Oriented Real-Time Distributed Computing (ISORC 2001)*, Magdeburg, Germany, pp. 69–76, May 2001.

[GRA 69] GRAHAM R.L., "Bounds on multiprocessing timing anomalies", *SIAM Journal on Applied Mathematics*, vol. 17, no. 2, pp. 416–429, 1969.

[GRU 96] GRUNEWALD W., UNGERER T., "Towards extremely fast context switching in a block-multithreaded processor", *EUROMICRO Conference*, vol. 0, p. 0592, IEEE Computer Society, pp. 592–599, 1996.

[GRU 10a] GRUND D., REINEKE J., "Precise and efficient FIFO-replacement analysis based on static phase detection", *Euromicro Conference on Real-Time Systems (ECRTS)*, 2010.

[GRU 10b] GRUND D., REINEKE J., "Toward precise PLRU cache analyis", *International Workshop on WCET Analysis*, 2010.

[GRU 11a] GRUND D., REINEKE J., GEBHARD G., "Branch target buffers: WCET analysis framework and timing predictability", *Journal of Systems Architecture*, vol. 57, no. 6, pp. 625–637, 2011.

[GRU 11b] GRUND D., REINEKE J., WILHELM R., "A template for predictability definitions with supporting evidence", *Bringing Theory to Practice: Predictability and Performance in Embedded Systems (Workshop)*, Schloss Dagstuhl, Germany, pp. 22–31, 2011.

[GUS 06] GUSTAFSSON J., ERMEDAHL A., SANDBERG C., *et al.*, "Automatic derivation of loop bounds and infeasible paths for WCET analysis using abstract execution", *27th IEEE International Real-Time Systems Symposium, 2006 (RTSS '06)*, IEEE, Rio de Janeiro, Brazil, pp. 57–66, 2006.

[GUS 09] GUSTAFSSON J., ERMEDAHL A., LISPER B., *et al.*, "ALF–a language for WCET flow analysis", *Proceedings of the 9th International Workshop on Worst-Case Execution Time Analysis (WCET 2009)*, Dublin, Ireland, pp. 1–11, 2009.

[GUS 10] GUSTAFSSON J., BETTS A., ERMEDAHL A., *et al.*, "The Mälardalen WCET benchmarks: past, present and future", *International Workshop on WCET Analysis*, Brussels, Belgium, 2010.

[HAN 99] HANGAL S., O'CONNOR M., "Performance analysis and validation of the picoJava processor", *IEEE Micro*, vol. 19, pp. 66–72, 1999.

[HAR 08] HARDY D., PUAUT I., "WCET analysis of multi-level non-inclusive set-associative instruction caches", *Real-Time Systems Symposium (RTSS)*, Barcelona, Spain, 2008.

[HAR 09a] HARDAVELLAS N., FERDMAN M., FALSAFI B., *et al.*, "Reactive NUCA: near-optimal block placement and replication in distributed caches", *Proceedings of the 36th Annual International Symposium on Computer Architecture, (ISCA '09)*, ACM, New York, NY, pp. 184–195, Austin, USA, 2009.

[HAR 09b] HARDAVELLAS N., FERDMAN M., FALSAFI B., *et al.*, "Reactive NUCA: near-optimal block placement and replication in distributed caches", *SIGARCH Computer Architecture News*, vol. 37, no. 3, pp. 184–195, June 2009.

[HAR 09c] HARDY D., PIQUET T., PUAUT I., "Using bypass to tighten WCET estimates for multi-core processors with shared instruction caches", *30th IEEE Real-Time Systems Symposium, 2009 (RTSS 2009)*, IEEE, pp. 68–77, Washington, USA, 2009.

[HEA 00] HEALY C., SJÖDIN M., RUSTAGI V., *et al.*, "Supporting timing analysis by automatic bounding of loop iterations", *Real-Time Systems*, vol. 18, no. 2–3, pp. 129–156, 2000.

[HEC 03] HECKMANN R., LANGENBACH M., THESING S., *et al.*, "The influence of processor architecture on the design and the results of WCET tools", *Proceedings of the IEEE*, vol. 91, pp. 1038–1054, 2003.

[HEN 07] HENNESSY J.L., PATTERSON D.A., *Computer Architecture – A Quantitative Approach*, 4th ed., Morgan Kaufmann, San Francisco, USA, 2007.

[HOL 07] HOLSTI N., "Analysing switch-case tables by partial evaluation", *7th Workshop on WCET Analysis*, Prague, Czech Republic, 2007.

[HUB 09] HUBER B., SCHOEBERL M., "Comparison of implicit path enumeration and model checking based WCET analysis", *Proceedings of the 9th International Workshop on Worst-Case Execution Time (WCET) Analysis*, pp. 23–34, Dublin, Ireland, 2009.

[HUY 11] HUYNH B.K., JU L., ROYCHOUDHURY A., "Scope-aware data cache analysis for WCET estimation", *Real-Time and Embedded Technology and Applications Symposium (RTAS)*, Chicago, USA, 2011.

[INF] INFINEON TECHNOLOGIES AG, TriCore 2,32-bit unified processor core v2.0 architecture, Infineon technologies, June 2003, Available at http://www.infineon.com/cms/de/product/channel.html?channel=db3a304312bae05f0112be54d22c00e6.

[INF 08] INFINEON TECHNOLOGIES AG, TriCore 1 32-bit unified processor core user's manual, V1.3.8, January 2008.

[JER 08] JERGER N.E., PEH L.-S., LIPASTI M., "Virtual circuit tree multicasting: a case for on-chip hardware multicast support", *Proceedings of the 35th Annual International Symposium on Computer Architecture, (ISCA '08)*, IEEE Computer Society, Washington, DC, pp. 229–240, Beijing, China, 2008.

[KAS 12] KÄSTNER D., FERDINAND C., "Safety standards and WCET analysis tools", *Embedded Real Time Software and Systems Congress (ERTS2)*, Toulouse, France, 2012.

[KAT 85a] KATZ R.H., EGGERS S.J., WOOD D.A., *et al.*, "Implementing a cache consistency protocol", *Proceedings of the 12th Annual International Symposium on Computer Architecture, (ISCA '85)*, IEEE Computer Society Press, Los Alamitos, CA, pp. 276–283, Boston, USA, 1985.

[KAT 85b] KATZ R.H., EGGERS S.J., WOOD D.A., *et al.*, "Implementing a cache consistency protocol", *SIGARCH Computer Architecture News*, vol. 13, no. 3, pp. 276–283, June 1985.

[KEL 10] KELM J.H., JOHNSON D.R., TUOHY W., *et al.*, "Cohesion: a hybrid memory model for accelerators", *Proceedings of the 37th Annual International Symposium on Computer Architecture, (ISCA '10)*, ACM, New York, NY, pp. 429–440, Saint-Malo, France, 2010.

[KIR 07] KIRNER R., KNOOP J., PRANTL A., *et al.*, "WCET analysis: the annotation language challenge", *7th International Workshop on WorstCase Execution Time Analysis*, Institut de Recherche en Informatique de Toulouse, pp. 83–99, 2007.

[KIR 09] KIRNER R., KADLEC A., PUSCHNER P., "Precise worst-case execution time analysis for processors with timing anomalies", *21st Euromicro Conference on Real-Time Systems, 2009 (ECRTS'09)*, IEEE, pp. 119–128, Dublin, Ireland, 2009.

[KNO 12] KNOOP J., KOVÁCS L., ZWIRCHMAYR J., "r-TuBound: loop bounds for WCET nalysis (tool paper)", *Logic for Programming, Artificial Intelligence, and Reasoning*, Springer, pp. 435–444, 2012.

[KRE 00a] KREUZINGER J., PFEFFER M., SCHULZ A., *et al.*, "Performance evaluations of a multithreaded Java microcontroller", *International Conference on Parallel and Distributed Processing Techniques and Applications (PDPTA)*, Las Vegas, NV, pp. 95–99, June 2000.

[KRE 00b] KREUZINGER J., SCHULZ A., PFEFFER M., *et al.*, "Real-time scheduling on multithreaded processors", *7th International Conference on Real-Time Computing Systems and Applications (RTCSA 2000)*, Cheju Island, South Korea, pp. 155–159, December 2000.

[LEE 98] LEE C.-G., HAHN H., SEO Y.-M., *et al.*, "Analysis of cache-related preemption delay in fixed-priority preemptive scheduling", *IEEE Transactions on Computers*, vol. 47, no. 6, pp. 700–713, 1998.

[LES 09] LESAGE B., HARDY D., PUAUT I., *et al.*, "WCET analysis of multi-level set-associative data caches", *International Workshop on WCET Analysis*, Dublin, Ireland, 2009.

[LES 10] LESAGE B., HARDY D., PUAUT I., *et al.*, "Shared data caches conflicts reduction for WCET computation in multi-core architectures", *18th International Conference on Real-Time and Network Systems*, Toulouse, France, 2010.

[LEU 82] LEUNG J.Y.-T., WHITEHEAD J., "On the complexity of fixed-priority scheduling of periodic, real-time tasks", *Performance evaluation*, vol. 2, no. 4, pp. 237–250, 1982.

[LI 95a] LI Y.-T.S., MALIK S., "Performance analysis of embedded software using implicit path enumeration", *ACM SIGPLAN Notices*, vol. 30, pp. 88–98, 1995.

[LI 95b] LI Y.-T.S., MALIK S., WOLFE A., "Performance estimation of embedded software with instruction cache modeling", *International Conference on Computer-Aided Design (ICCAD)*, San Jose, USA, 1995.

[LI 05] LI X., MITRA T., ROYCHOUDHURY A., "Modeling control speculation for timing analysis", *Real-Time Systems*, vol. 29, no. 1, pp. 27–58, 2005.

[LI 06] LI X., ROYCHOUDHURY A., MITRA T., "Modeling out-of-order processors for WCET analysis", *Journal of Real-Time Systems*, vol. 34, no. 3, pp. 195–227, 2006.

[LI 07] LI X., LIANG Y., MITRA T., *et al.*, "Chronos: a timing analyzer for embedded software", *Science of Computer Programming*, vol. 69, no. 1–3, pp. 56–67, 2007.

[LI 09] LI Y., SUHENDRA V., LIANG Y., *et al.*, "Timing analysis of concurrent programs running on shared cache multi-cores", *30th IEEE Real-Time Systems Symposium, 2009, (RTSS 2009)*, IEEE, pp. 57–67, Washington, USA, 2009.

[LIC 08] LICKLY B., LIU I., KIM S., *et al.*, "Predictable programming on a precision timed architecture", *Proceedings of the 2008 International Conference on Compilers, Architectures and Synthesis for Embedded Systems*, ACM, pp. 137–146, Atlanta, USA, 2008.

[LIM 95] LIM S.-S., BAE Y.H., JANG G.T., *et al.*, "An accurate worst case timing analysis for RISC processors", *IEEE Transactions on Software Engineering*, vol. 21, no. 7, pp. 593–604, 1995.

[LIM 98] LIM S.-S., KIM J., MIN S.L., "A worst case timing analysis technique for optimized programs", *Proceedings of the 5th International Conference on Real-Time Computing Systems and Applications, 1998*, IEEE, pp. 151–157, Hiroshima, Japan, 1998.

[LIU 73] LIU C.L., LAYLAND J.W., "Scheduling algorithms for multiprogramming in a hard-real-time environment", *Journal of the ACM*, vol. 20, no. 1, pp. 46–61, January 1973.

[LIU 09] LIU T., LI M., XUE C.J., "Minimizing WCET for real-time embedded systems via static instruction cache locking", *Real-Time and Embedded Technology and Applications Symposium (RTAS)*, San Francisco, USA, 2009.

[LIU 10] LIU I., REINEKE J., LEE E., "A PRET architecture supporting concurrent programs with composable timing properties", *2010 Conference Record of the Forty Fourth Asilomar Conference on Signals, Systems and Computers (ASILOMAR)*, IEEE, Pacific Grove, USA, pp. 2111–2115, November 2010.

[LUN 99a] LUNDQVIST T., STENSTRÖM P., "An integrated path and timing analysis method based on cycle-level symbolic execution", *Real-Time Systems*, vol. 17, no. 2, pp. 183–207, 1999.

[LUN 99b] LUNDQVIST T., STENSTROM P., "Timing anomalies in dynamically scheduled microprocessors", *Real-Time Systems Symposium (RTSS)*, IEEE, pp. 12–21, Phoenix, USA, 1999.

[LUN 12] LUNNISS W., ALTMEYER S., DAVIS R.I., "Optimising task layout to increase schedulability via reduced cache related pre-emption delays", *International Conference on Real-Time Networks and Systems (RTNS)*, Pont-à-Mousson, France, 2012.

[LUN 13] LUNNISS W., DAVIS R.I., ALTMEYER S., *et al.*, "Integrating cache related preemption delay analysis into EDF scheduling", *Real-Time and Embedded Technology and Applications Symposium (RTAS)*, 2013.

[MAA 91] MAA Y.-C., PRADHAN D.K., THIEBAUT D., "Two economical directory schemes for large-scale cache coherent multiprocessors", *SIGARCH Computer Architecture News*, vol. 19, no. 5, pp. 10, September pp. 10–18, 1991.

[MAI 11] MAÏZA C., ROCHANGE C., "A framework for the timing analysis of dynamic branch predictors (regular paper)", *International Conference on Real-Time Networks and Systems (RTNS)*, Nantes, France, 2011.

[MET 04] METZNER A., "Why model checking can improve WCET analysis", *16th Conf. on Computer Aided Verification*, Springer, pp. 334–347, Boston, USA, 2004.

[MET 08] METZLAFF S., UHRIG S., MISCHE J., *et al.*, "Predictable dynamic instruction scratchpad for simultaneous multithreaded processors", *Proceedings of the 9th Workshop on Memory Performance (MEDEA '08)*, ACM, New York, NY pp. 38–45, Toronto, Canada, 2008.

[MET 12] METZLAFF S., UNGERER T., "Impact of instruction cache and different instruction scratchpads on the WCET estimate", *Proceedings of the 9th International Conference on Embedded Software and Systems (ICESS)*, Liverpool, UK, pp. 1442–1449, 2012.

[MIN 92] MIN S.L., BAER J.L., "Design and analysis of a scalable cache coherence scheme based on clocks and timestamps", *IEEE Transactions on Parallel and Distributed System*, vol. 3, no. 1, pp. 25–44, January 1992.

[MIP 09] MIPS TECHNOLOGIES, INC., "*MIPS32 Architecture For Programmers, Volume II: The MIPS32 Instruction Set*", MIPS Technologies, Mountain View, CA, January 2009.

[MIS 09] MISCHE J., UHRIG S., KLUGE F., *et al.*, "IPC control for multiple real-time threads on an in-order SMT processor", *Proceedings of the 4th International Conference on High Performance and Embedded Architectures and Compilers (HiPEAC 2009)*, Paphos, Cyprus, pp. 125–139, January 2009.

[MIS 10a] MISCHE J., GULIASHVILI I., UHRIG S., *et al.*, "How to enhance a superscalar processor to provide hard real-time capable in-order smt", *Architecture of Computing Systems-ARCS 2010*, Springer, pp. 2–14, 2010.

[MIS 10b] MISCHE J., GULIASHVILI I., UHRIG S., *et al.*, "How to enhance a superscalar processor to provide hard real-time capable in-order SMT", *International Conference on Architecture of Computing Systems (ARCS 2010)*, Springer, Prague, Czech Republic, pp. 2–14, February 2010.

[MIS 10c] MISCHE J., UHRIG S., KLUGE F., *et al.*, "Using SMT to hide context switch times of large real-time tasksets", *The 16th IEEE International Conference on Embedded and Real-Time Computing Systems and Applications (RTCSA 2010)*, Macau, China, August 2010.

[MOL 06] MOLNOS A.M., COTOFANA S.D., HEIJLIGERS M.J., *et al.*, "Throughput optimization via cache partitioning for embedded multiprocessors", *International Conference on Embedded Computer Systems: Architectures, Modeling and Simulation, 2006 (IC-SAMOS 2006)*, pp. 185–191, Samos, Greece, July 2006.

[MOO 04] MOON B.I., YOON H., YUN I., *et al.*, "An in-order SMT architecture with static resource partitoning for consumer applications", *Parallel and Distributed Computing: Applications and Technologies, LNCS 3320*, Springer-Verlag, pp. 539–544, 2004.

[MUE 95] MUELLER F., WHALLEY D.B., "Fast instruction cache analysis via static cache simulation", *Annual Simulation Symposium*, Santa Barbara, USA, 1995.

[O'KR 90] O'KRAFKA B.W., NEWTON A.R., "An empirical evaluation of two memory-efficient directory methods", *Proceedings of the 17th Annual International Symposium on Computer Architecture, (ISCA '90)*, ACM, New York, NY, pp. 138–147, Seattle, USA, 1990.

[OZA 09] OZAKTAS H., HEYDEMANN K., ROCHANGE C., *et al.*, "Impact of code compression on estimated worst-case execution times", *17th International Conference on Real-Time and Network Systems*, INRIA, Paris, France, pp. 55–66, 2009.

[PAN 96] PAN D., "A tutorial on MPEG/audio compression", *IEEE MultiMedia*, vol. 2, pp. 60–74, 1996.

[PAO 09a] PAOLIERI M., QUIÑONES E., CAZORLA F.J., *et al.*, "Hardware support for WCET analysis of hard real-time multicore systems", *ACM SIGARCH Computer Architecture News*, vol. 37, pp. 57–68, 2009.

[PAO 09b] PAOLIERI M., QUIÑONES E., CAZORLA F.J., *et al.*, "An analyzable memory controller for hard real-time CMPs", *IEEE Embedded Systems Letters*, vol. 1, no. 4, pp. 86–90, 2009.

[PAP 84] PAPAMARCOS M.S., PATEL J.H., "A low-overhead coherence solution for multiprocessors with private cache memories", *Proceedings of the 11th Annual International Symposium on Computer Architecture, (ISCA '84)*, ACM, New York, NY, pp. 348–354, Ann Arbor, USA, 1984.

[PAR 11] PARK J., JANG C., LEE J., "A software-managed coherent memory architecture for manycores", *Proceedings of the 2011 International Conference on Parallel Architectures and Compilation Techniques, (PACT '11)*, IEEE Computer Society, Washington, DC, p. 213, Galueston Island, USA, 2011.

[PLA 09] PLAZAR S., LOKUCIEJEWSKI P., MARWEDEL P., "WCET-aware software based cache partitioning for multi-task real-time systems", *Proceedings of the 9th International Workshop on Worst-Case Execution Time Analysis (WCET)*, Austrian Computer Society, Dublin Ireland, pp. 78–88, 2009.

[PLA 12] PLAZAR S., KLEINSORGE J.C., MARWEDEL P., *et al.*, "WCET-aware static locking of instruction caches", *10th International Symposium on Code Generation and Optimization (CGO)*, ACM, San Jose, USA, pp. 44–52, 2012.

[POP 04] POPOVIC R.S., *Hall Effect Devices*, 2nd ed., Institute of Physics Publishing, London, UK, 2004.

[PUA 02a] PUAUT I., DECOTIGNY D., "Low-complexity algorithms for static cache locking in multitasking hard real-time systems", *Real-Time Systems Symposium (RTSS)*, IEEE, Austin, USA, pp. 114–123, 2002.

[PUA 02b] PUAUT I., DECOTIGNY D., "Low-complexity algorithms for static cache locking in multitasking hard real-time systems", *23rd IEEE Real-Time Systems Symposium, 2002 (RTSS 2002)* , IEEE, Austin, USA, pp. 114–123, 2002.

[PUA 06a] PUAUT I., "WCET-centric software-controlled instruction caches for hard real-time systems", *18th Euromicro Conference on Real-Time Systems (ECRTS)*, IEEE, Dresden, Germany, 2006.

[PUA 06b] PUAUT I., "WCET-centric software-controlled instruction caches for hard real-time systems", *18th Euromicro Conference on Real-Time Systems, 2006*, IEEE, Dresden, Germany, pp. 217–226, 2006.

[PUS 89] PUSCHNER P., KOZA C., "Calculating the maximum execution time of real-time programs", *Real-Time Systems*, vol. 1, no. 2, pp. 159–176, 1989.

[PUS 02] PUSCHNER P., BURNS A., "Writing temporally predictable code", *Proceedings of the Seventh International Workshop on Object-Oriented Real-Time Dependable Systems, 2002 (WORDS 2002)*, IEEE, San Diego, USA, pp. 85–91, 2002.

[PUS 03] PUSCHNER P., "The single-path approach towards WCET-analysable software", *IEEE International Conference on Industrial Technology*, vol. 2, Maribor, Slovenia, pp. 699–704, 2003.

[QUE 82] QUEILLE J., SIFAKIS J., "Specification and verification of concurrent systems in CESAR", *International Symposium on Programming*, Turin, Italy, 1982.

[RAP 09] RAPITA SYSTEMS LTD., "RapiTime product brochure", 2009. Available at http://www.rapitasystems.com/system/files/ RapiTimeBrochure.pdf.

[RED 07] REDDY R., PETROV P., "Eliminating inter-process cache interference through cache reconfigurability for real-time and low-power embedded multi-tasking systems", *Proceedings of the 2007 International Conference on Compilers, Architecture, and Synthesis for Embedded Systems*, ACM, Salzburg, Austria, pp. 198–207, 2007.

[REG 05] REGEHR J., REID A., WEBB K., "Eliminating stack overflow by abstract interpretation", *ACM Transactions on Embedded Computing Systems (TECS)*, vol. 4, no. 4, pp. 751–778, 2005.

[REI 06] REINEKE J., WACHTER B., THESING S., *et al.*, "A definition and classification of timing anomalies", *6th International Workshop on Worst-Case Execution Time Analysis*, Dresden, Germany, 2006.

[REI 07] REINEKE J., GRUND D., BERG C., *et al.*, "Timing Predictability of cache replacement policies", *Real-Time Systems*, vol. 37, no. 2, pp. 99–122, 2007.

[REI 09] REINEKE J., SEN R., "Sound and efficient WCET analysis in the presence of timing anomalies", *9th International Workshop on Worst-Case Execution Time Analysis*, Austrian Computer Society, Dublin, Ireland, pp. 1–11, 2009.

[REI 11] REINEKE J., LIU I., PATEL H.D., *et al.*, "PRET DRAM controller: bank privatization for predictability and temporal isolation", *Proceedings of the 7th IEEE/ACM/IFIP International Conference on Hardware/Software Codesign and System Synthesis (CODES+ISSS '11)*, ACM, Montreal, Canada, pp. 99–108, October 2011.

[REI 13] REINEKE J., GRUND D., "Sensitivity of cache replacement policies", *ACM Transactions on Embedded Computing Systems (TECS)*, vol. 12, no. 1, pp. 42:1–42:18, 2013.

[ROC 05] ROCHANGE C., SAINRAT P., "A time-predictable execution mode for superscalar pipelines with instruction prescheduling", *Proceedings of the 2nd Conference on Computing Frontiers (CF '05)*, ACM, New York, NY, pp. 307–314, Ischia, Italy, 2005.

[ROC 09] ROCHANGE C., SAINRAT P., "A context-parameterized model for static analysis of execution times", *Transactions on High-Performance Embedded Architectures and Compilers II*, pp. 222–241, 2009.

[ROC 10] ROCHANGE C., BONENFANT A., SAINRAT P., *et al.*, "WCET analysis of a parallel 3D multigrid solver executed on the MERASA multi-core", in LISPER B. (ed.), *10th International Workshop on Worst-Case Execution Time Analysis (WCET 2010)*, vol. 15 of *OpenAccess Series in Informatics (OASIcs)*, Schloss Dagstuhl–Leibniz-Zentrum fuer Informatik, Dagstuhl, Germany, pp. 90–100, Brussels Belgium, 2010.

[ROS 07] ROSEN J., ANDREI A., ELES P., *et al.*, "Bus access optimization for predictable implementation of real-time applications on multiprocessor systems-on-chip", *28th IEEE International Real-Time Systems Symposium, 2007 (RTSS 2007)*, IEEE, Tucson, USA, pp. 49–60, 2007.

[ROS 12] ROS A., KAXIRAS S., "Complexity-effective multicore coherence", *Proceedings of the 21st International Conference on Parallel Architectures and Compilation Techniques, (PACT '12)*, ACM, New York, NY, pp. 241–252, Minneapolis, USA, 2012.

[SAL 75] SALE A.H.J., The basic principles of well-structured code, PhD Thesis, Australian Computer Society Inc., 1975.

[SCH 08] SCHOEBERL M., "JOP," 2008. Available at http://www.jopdesign.com/.

[SCH 99] SCHNEIDER J., FERDINAND C., "Pipeline behavior prediction for superscalar processors by abstract interpretation", *ACM SIGPLAN Notices*, vol. 34, no. 7, pp. 35–44, 1999.

[SCH 04a] SCHOEBERL M., "Real-time scheduling on a Java processor", *Proceedings of the 10th International Conference on Real-Time and Embedded Computing Systems and Applications (RTCSA 2004)*, Gothenburg, Sweden, August 2004.

[SCH 04b] SCHOEBERL M., "A time predictable instruction cache for a Java processor", *On the Move to Meaningful Internet Systems 2004: Workshop on Java Technologies for Real-Time and Embedded Systems (JTRES 2004)*, vol. 3292 of LNCS, Springer, Ayia Napa, Cyprus, pp. 371–382, October 2004.

[SCH 06] SCHOEBERL M., "Real-time garbage collection for Java", *Proceedings of the 9th IEEE International Symposium on Object and Component-Oriented Real-Time Distributed Computing (ISORC 2006)*, Gyeongju, Korea, pp. 424–432, April 2006.

[SCH 08] SCHOEBERL M., "A Java processor architecture for embedded real-time systems", *Journal of Systems Architecture*, vol. 54/1–2, pp. 265–286, 2008.

[SCH 09a] SCHOEBERL M., *JOP Reference Handbook*, CreateSpace, 2009.

[SCH 09b] SCHOEBERL M., "Time-predictable computer architecture", *EURASIP Journal on Embedded Systems*, vol. 29, pp. 1–17, 2009.

[SCH 10] SCHLICKLING M., PISTER M., "Semi-automatic derivation of timing models for WCET analysis", *ACM Sigplan Notices*, vol. 45, pp. 67–76, 2010.

[SCH 11] SCHOEBERL M., SCHLEUNIGER P., PUFFITSCH W., *et al.*, *Bringing Theory to Practice: Predictability and Performance in Embedded Systems*, pp. 11–21, OASICS, 2011.

[SCH 12] SCHOEBERL M., BRANDNER F., SPARSØ J., KASAPAKI E., "A statically scheduled time-division-multiplexed network-on-chip for real-time systems", *Proceedings of the 6th International Symposium on Networks-on-Chip (NOCS)*, IEEE, Lyngby, Denmark, pp. 152–160, 2012.

[SEN 07] SEN R., SRIKANT Y., "WCET estimation for executables in the presence of data caches", *International Conference on Embedded Software (EMSOFT)*, Salzburg, Austria, 2007.

[SHA 89] SHAW A.C., "Reasoning about time in higher-level language software", *IEEE Transactions on Software Engineering*, vol. 15, no. 7, pp. 875–889, 1989.

[SIF 01] SIFAKIS J., "Modeling real-time systems – challenges and work directions", *International Conference on Embedded Software (EMSOFT)*, Lake Tahoe, USA, 2001.

[SON 10] SONDAG T., RAJAN H., "A more precise abstract domain for multi-level caches for tighter wcet analysis", *Real-Time Systems Symposium (RTSS)*, San Diego, USA, 2010.

[SOU 05] SOUYRIS J., LE PAVEC E., HIMBERT G., *et al.*, "Computing the worst case execution time of an avionics program by abstract interpretation", *Proceedings of the 5th International Workshop on Worst-Case Execution Time (WCET) Analysis*, 2005.

[SPA 10] SPANSION LLC, S29CD-J and S29CL-J Flash Family. Available at http://www.spansion.com/Support/Datasheets/S29CD-J_CL-J_00.pdf.

[SPU 96] SPURI M., BUTTAZZO G., "Scheduling aperiodic tasks in dynamic priority systems", *Real-Time Systems*, vol. 10, no. 2, pp. 179–210, 1996.

[STA 98] STANKOVIC J.A., SPURI M., RAMAMRITHMA K., *et al.*, *Deadline Scheduling for Real-Time Systems: EDF and Related Algorithms*, Springer, 1998.

[STE 90] STENSTROM P., "A survey of cache coherence schemes for multiprocessors", *IEEE Computer*, vol. 23, no. 6, pp. 12–24, June 1990.

[STE 07] STEIN I., MARTIN F., "Analysis of path exclusion at the machine code level", *7th International Workshop on Worst-Case Execution-Time Analysis*, vol. 24, Prague, Czech Republic, 2007.

[SUD 04] SUDARSHAN T., MIR R.A., VIJAYALAKSHMI S., "Highly efficient LRU implementations for high associativity cache memory", *Proceedings of the 12th IEEE International Conference on Advanced Computing and Communications*, Allied Publishers Pvt. Ltd., Ahmedabad, India (ADCOM), pp. 87–95, 2004.

[SUH 05] SUHENDRA V., MITRA T., ROYCHOUDHURY A., *et al.*, "WCET centric data allocation to scratchpad memory", *Real-Time Systems Symposium (RTSS)*, IEEE, Miami, USA, 2005.

[SUH 08] SUHENDRA V., MITRA T., "Exploring locking & partitioning for predictable shared caches on multi-cores", *Proceedings of the 45th Annual Design Automation Conference*, ACM, pp. 300–303, Anaheim, USA, 2008.

[TAN 07] TAN Y., MOONEY V., "Timing analysis for preemptive multitasking real-time systems with caches", *ACM Transactions on Embedded Computing Systems (TECS)*, vol. 6, no. 1, pp. 7:1–7:29, 2007.

[THA 87] THACKER C.P., STEWART L.C., "Firefly: a multiprocessor workstation", *Proceedings of the 2nd International Conference on Architectual Support for Programming Languages and Operating Systems*, ASPLOS-II, IEEE Computer Society Press, Los Alamitos, CA, pp. 164–172, Palo Alto, USA, 1987.

[THA 90] THAPAR M., DELAGI B., "Stanford distributed-directory protocol", *Computer*, vol. 23, no. 6, pp. 78–80, June 1990.

[THE 04] THESING S., Safe and precise worst-case execution time prediction by abstract interpretation of pipeline models, PhD Thesis, University of Saarland, Germany, 2004.

[THU 94] THUEL S.R., LEHOCZKY J.P., "Algorithms for scheduling hard aperiodic tasks in fixed-priority systems using slack stealing", *Real-Time Systems Symposium*, IEEE, pp. 22–33, San Juan, Puerto Rico, 1994.

[TOM 94] TOMASEVIC M., MILUTINOVIC V., "Hardware approaches to cache coherence in shared-memory multiprocessors Part 2", *IEEE Micro*, vol. 14, no. 6, pp. 61–66, December 1994.

[TUL 96a] TULLSEN D.M., "Simulation and modeling of a simultaneous multithreading processor", *22nd Annual Computer Measurement Group Conference*, San Diego, USA, December 1996.

[TUL 96b] TULLSEN D.M., EGGERS S.J., EMER J.S., *et al.*, "Exploiting choice: instruction fetch and issue on an implementable simultaneous multithreading processor", *23rd International Symposium on Computer Architecture (ISCA 1996), Philadelphia, PA*, pp. 191–202, May 1996.

[UHR 07a] UHRIG S., MISCHE J., UNGERER T., "An IP core for embedded Java systems", *Proceedings of the 7th International Conference on Embedded Computer Systems (SAMOS '07)*, Springer-Verlag, Berlin, Heidelberg, pp. 263–272, Samos, Greece, 2007.

[UHR 07b] UHRIG S., WIESE J., "jamuth: an IP processor core for embedded Java real-time systems", *Proceedings of the 5th International Workshop on Java Technologies for Real-Time and Embedded Systems (JTRES '07)*, ACM, Vienna, Austria, pp. 230–237, 2007.

[UHR 08] UHRIG S., "A flexible Java-on-chip solution (Eine flexible Java-on-Chip Lösung)", *IT – Information Technology*, vol. 50, no. 5, pp. 317–323, 2008.

[UHR 09a] UHRIG S., "Evaluation of different multithreaded and multicore processor configurations for SoPC", *Embedded Computer Systems: Architectures, Modeling, and Simulation*, vol. 5657 of Lecture Notes in Computer Science, Springer, Berlin/Heidelberg, pp. 68–77, 2009.

[UHR 09b] UHRIG S., "A garbage collection technique for embedded multithreaded multicore processors", *International Conference on Architecture of Computing Systems (ARCS 2009)*, vol. 5455 of Lecture Notes in Computer Science, Springer, Berlin/Heidelberg, pp. 207–218, Delft, The Netherlands, 2009.

[UNG 03] UNGERER T., ROBIC B., SILC J., "A survey of processors with explicit multithreading", *ACM Computing Surveys*, vol. 35, no. 1, pp. 29–63, 2003.

[UNG 10] UNGERER T., CAZORLA F.J., SAINRAT P., *et al.*, "MERASA: multi-core execution of hard real-time applications supporting analysability", *IEEE Micro Special Issue on European Multicore Computing Projects* vol 30, no. 5, pp. 66–75, 2010.

[VER 03] VERA X., LISPER B., XUE J., "Data cache locking for higher program predictability", *SIGMETRICS Performance Evaluation Review*, vol. 31, no. 1, pp. 272–282, 2003.

[VON 11] VON HANXLEDEN R., HOLSTI N., LISPER B., *et al.*, "WCET tool challenge 2011: report", *Proceedings of the 11th International Workshop on Worst-Case Execution Time (WCET) Analysis*, Porto, Portugal, 2011.

[WEA 94] WEAVER D.L., GERMOND T., *The SPARC Architecture Manual*, PTR Prentice Hall, Englewood Cliffs, NJ, 1994.

[WEG 98] WEGENER J., GROCHTMANN M., "Verifying timing constraints of real-time systems by means of evolutionary testing", *Real-Time Systems*, vol. 15, no. 3, pp. 275–298, 1998.

[WEN 05] WENZEL I., KIRNER R., PUSCHNER P., *et al.*, "Principles of timing anomalies in superscalar processors", *Proceedings of the 5th International Conference on Quality Software (QSIC '05)*, IEEE Computer Society, Washington, DC, pp. 295–306, Melbourne, Australia, 2005.

[WIL 09] WILLIAMS N., ROGER M., "Test generation strategies to measure worst-case execution time", *4th International Workshop on Automation of Software Test (AST)*, Vancouver, Canada, 2009.

[YAN 08] YAN J., ZHANG W., "WCET analysis for multi-core processors with shared L2 instruction caches", *Real-Time and Embedded Technology and Applications Symposium (RTAS '08)*, IEEE, St. Louis, USA, pp. 80–89, 2008.

[ZAB 09] ZABEL M., SPALLEK R.G., SHAP – scalable multi-core Java bytecode processor, Report , Faculty of computer science, Technical University of Dresden, 2009. Available at ftp://ftp.inf.tu-dresden.de/pub/berichte/tud09-13.pdf.

[ZEB 07] ZEBCHUK J., SAFI E., MOSHOVOS A., "A framework for coarse-grain optimizations in the on-chip memory hierarchy", *Proceedings of the 40th Annual IEEE/ACM International Symposium on Microarchitecture*, MICRO 40, IEEE Computer Society, Washington, DC, pp. 314–327, Chicago, USA, 2007.

[ZHO 10] ZHOU X., CHEN H., LUO S., *et al.*, "A case for software managed coherence in many-core processors", *Proceedings of the 2nd Usenix Workshop on Hot Topics in Parallelism*, Usenix Association, Berkeley, USA, 2010.

Index